BURGER
BRILLIANCE

The Recipe of Innovation, Insight & Imagination
Wells Cattle Co. Burgers & Pies

Lee E. Wells

WELLS RANCH
PUBLISHING COMPANY

DEDICATION

This book is dedicated to my late father, Keith E. Wells, who never gave up on anything or anyone. Thank you for teaching me so much over the years, both spoken and observed. This book is written in your loving memory.

I also dedicate this book to the hard-working entrepreneurs who wake up every morning excited to take on the inevitable challenges they are sure to face to see their dreams come true.

THANK YOU

I must thank a few people who made this book possible. Without each of you, it would have been much harder to complete, maybe even impossible to begin. To my wonderful wife, Lynda, and my sweet girls, Kayla and Addison, thank you for putting up with me during this season of needing the room quiet when you came in from your day. To Clayton, my right hand on the ranch, thank you for taking care of things all those mornings I was late coming out of the house. To my mom, Judy, thank you for all the "English teacher raising" you did for me growing up. Who would have thought this son would have ever written a book? Thank you for editing this manuscript and working all those hours to help smooth out the *country boy talkin'* that was originally there. To the amazing beta readers who used their precious time to pre-read my manuscript and give valuable feedback, especially, Ron Gray, for the extra effort that you put into this project with me. I will always be grateful for your meticulous perfection. Also, to my talented friend Radovan Hajduk, your illustrations bring life to the words on the page perfectly. To Michelle Prince for your expertise in publishing. Thank you for helping me get to the finish line! Finally, to my Lord Jesus for allowing me the ability to put two sentences together and the grace to live long enough to share those few sentences with others. I owe everything to Your healing hand leading my life.

I truly enjoyed this book! I felt as if Lee were writing the book to me personally, expressing many of the same feelings we share in the restaurant business. He touched upon the two most important elements in the business that are not discussed enough, culture and restaurant image. I hope customers of the restaurant industry can grasp an idea of how much sweat, work, and tears go into the operation of a restaurant. I truly believe that a wholesale change may be needed in the restaurant industry and love that Lee lays out a plan to begin this process. I'm thoroughly impressed!

- Kevin Lefere, Partner & Head Chef, Zanata

Simply put, this book is for everyone. You can use the following pages to activate memories, to remind you of good business practices, to motivate you to do better, or to simply read a story about one very driven and successful business owner. This is Lee's story, and you should read it.

- Jimmy Niwa, Owner, Niwa Japanese BBQ

What can you learn from a cowboy that runs a burger joint? Nothing much, right? You'd be wrong! Wells captures the highs and lows of operating a highly successful business in one of the most difficult industries in which to succeed. He provides a glimpse into the inspiration, vision, creation, and continued evolution of his restaurant.

- Kevin Fowler, Sr. VP, Independent Financial,

Former Mayor, City of Rockwall, Texas

Burger Brilliance highlights experiences that helped shape my friend, Lee Wells, into the successful restaurateur that he is today. He lives his life openly and authentically and has a passion for serving others. I admire his faithfulness and commitment to the best quality and service. Lee's profound wisdom is what makes this book a great read for anyone wanting to be successful in the service industry.

- Chad Sessions, Owner, Smoke Sessions Barbecue

This book authentically embodies best practices in the food service industry. Lee's innovative ideas have weathered the most challenging times and consistently fostered sustainability and growth. Lee emphasizes a universal theme that serves as a perfect mantra, "You must serve with hospitality and love to prosper in this world."

- Brenda Meyers, CEO, Sterling Tea

Having known Lee almost all his life, it was a delight to read this book from a non-rancher and non-business owner point of view. It was a positive read from cover to cover. You will laugh and rejoice with a young man turned rancher and successful businessman enjoying the ride.

- Belinda McManus, Wells Customer

My wife and I have many favorite restaurants, but it wasn't until reading this book that the puzzle pieces fell into place. Now, we understand why we adore one restaurant over the other. It's all about the formula that Lee elucidates—a delicate balance of quality, service, and culture. We've always been told, "We eat with our eyes," but after reading this, you'll perceive sizzling fajitas in a whole new light.

- Mace & Shannon, Wells Customers

I found Lee's book to be a delightful, easy read. There is a lot of great advice that I agree with wholeheartedly. I found some good reminders and new ideas that I believe can be an asset to my own business!

- Cheri Stigler Owner & Executive Chef, Settler's Table

I loved this book. The lessons and takeaways it offers transcend the food and beverage world, with relevance to anything in which quality and excellence are a priority. It's a refreshing slice of Americana, full of concentrated and valuable content that is easily digestible and enjoyable. I can honestly speak very highly of this book, The Wells Cattle Co. restaurant and the food it consistently serves, and, of course, Lee.

- Brian Adams, Sr. VP, Food & Beverage Advisory, JLL

Lee is one of the few genuine and authentic men I know. He is hardworking and intelligent, with a heart to help everyone he can in order to share the blessings, knowledge, and wisdom he has learned from life experiences, as well as his family legacy. Lee is a cattle rancher, restaurant owner, and entrepreneur, as well as a man of deep faith. This book will teach you, encourage you, and inspire you to take a leap of faith. Wow! You'll want to step up and achieve your goals, dreams, and aspirations!

- Phillip Hatfield, Zig Ziglar Business Consultant & Keynote Speaker

In a world full of superficial, artificial, and mass-produced, people are hungry for authentic, genuine, and exceptional. What drew us to Wells and keeps us coming back is more than the delicious burgers; it is the real connection made with real people. *Burger Brilliance* isn't just about burgers. It's about being intentional with a true calling in life!

- David & Heather Poole, Wells Customers

I found Lee's book to be an enjoyable read. In addition to the brevity of the chapters, his style is easy to digest. As a former restaurant employee and frequent restaurant diner, I was surprised to learn how much thought and planning went into his restaurant... from the raising of the cattle to the dining experience. I won't spoil the book, but I have a renewed appreciation for a restaurant I've frequented many times since its opening. Y'all come to Rockwall and see for yourselves!

- Trace Johannesen, Mayor, City of Rockwall, Texas

CONTENTS

Wells Bacon Cheeseburger

CONTENTS

INTRODUCTION

THANK YOU FOR picking up this book. You may own it, or perhaps you are just perusing it, but I am grateful that you picked it up either way. This is my first attempt at book writing, and I really do not know much about this art form. I have read a few books, but authoring has proved to be a "whole other thing." My life stays busy with the ranch operation, the restaurant, church, and family. So, writing a book has not proved to be a luxury of time. It has, however, been a labor of passion. I love serving great customers and amazing food. I also love entrepreneurship and the intricacies of small business.

Much of the content in this book was written on an open document on my smartphone and typed with my two rapidly tapping thumbs. I truly hope you can appreciate the effort that has gone into this writing, and perhaps you will even overlook something that may not be said perfectly. I have also opted to publish a shorter book than some others. I have read books that took two pages to say what should have only taken a paragraph. It is possible that we are both running on a similar schedule, so fewer words cannot be a bad thing when it comes to available reading time.

This book is an opportunity to share some history about my company and operational concept, but it primarily explores the reasons we are successful and how we avoided several problem areas I see other restaurants and small businesses battling. At the time of this writing, we have maintained a 4.6-star review average on Google and a 4.5-star average on Yelp, with a combined total of almost two thousand reviews submitted to date. We have also won multiple "Best Burger" awards beginning the first year we opened and every year since. Our restaurant is located near some amazing restaurants in our area, many of them having specialty burgers on their menus. We are always immensely grateful for every recognition we receive. I say these things to help you quantify the purpose of the book and hope to convince you to spend some time considering the Wells way of thinking.

I hope my writing and opinions do not come across as sounding "holier-than-thou" in my approach to some of the tougher subjects. I am simply a country boy who has been lucky enough to get out and see some of the nation and then come home to try my hand at something I love: the hospitality and food business!

In two different careers, I was able to travel extensively, one on a corporate expense account and another as a public speaker, being treated to great dining experiences on a regular basis. I have always been a student of others, their behavior, and their successes. So even when I was not in the hospitality industry, I still observed those who were winning and those who were struggling. This may sound strange to some, but I am not impressed by expensive dinners or exclusive reservations. While traveling, I was always in search of the best food. Many times, local eateries that specialize in a specific style of cooking are unmatched by the finest chefs. And then, of course, there were mind-blowing dinners made by exclusive chefs as well.

Here is my baseline philosophy that we have used since opening our place: "If we can make people feel the way we want to feel when we sit down to eat, we can be successful." It does not really matter if you are in an exclusive dining venue owned by billionaires or in a mom-and-pop shop in a run-down part of town. When you are at someone else's table, you want to feel at home, comfortable, and relaxed. You want to feel welcome. It matters not if you are spending twenty dollars or two hundred dollars; you want to feel as if your money is well spent. How we strive to accomplish these objectives is what we discuss in the pages of this book.

I do hope you choose to read this book and that you find its content worthwhile. I believe that you will enjoy learning how we have built a multi-award-winning restaurant from our family ranch to our restaurant table.

Finally, I want you to know that I love and respect all people; and as random as that sounds right now, I hope that sentiment shows in this book. Taking care of each other is a paramount priority in life, and we have an amazing opportunity to help someone every time they walk through the door of our business. We do not know what people are going through in their lives. We cannot assume we understand their life and situation, so we want to make their time with us the best it can possibly be! Our business is about more than making a dollar, and I hope this mindset carries through to the page, even when it may sound like I am being critical of a practice within our industry. I never claim to own the keys to the restaurant business, but we have done some things very well, and we have done them on purpose. So, best wishes, and I hope you find something here to integrate into your life and business.

Lee E. Wells

FOREWORD

I MET LEE under unusual circumstances, in a helicopter. My first thoughts were that I had just met a real cowboy. Since I grew up in California, I did not think we would have much in common to talk about during the ride. Boy, was I wrong. I learned about Lee's program and his burgers. I will admit that I was skeptical about his approach to burgers, but after visiting Wells Cattle Co. Burgers & Pies one afternoon, I began to understand his concept. If you've met Lee in person, you know he's a passionate, empathetic, hardworking restaurant owner who cares more about quality burgers than anyone.

I have a huge amount of respect for the passion and dedication Lee has poured into his restaurant, and I am enjoying watching his success. His unique approach to burgers is a constant reminder to me that there is never just one way to do something, and that we can always do better.

Simply put, this book is for everyone. The choice is yours. You can use the following pages to activate memories, to remind you of good business practices, to motivate you to do better or to simply read a story about one very driven and successful restaurateur. Throughout these pages, Lee reminds us to strive to be the best while keeping a human approach. So much is lost from the corporate takeover of the farm to the table that you will be refreshed by the honesty and candor Lee provides.

Being involved in over forty restaurants during my career has allowed me to see the great, the not so great, and the downright dirty of the industry. Reading this book has brought inspiration and good memories back to me, as I hope it will to you. You will not find repetition or filler pages, as Lee gets right to the point with his direct approach. In our fast-paced industry as a restaurant owner or manager, we just do not have time to waste. My hat's off to you, Mr. Lee Wells. Very well put.

- Jimmy Niwa, Owner, Niwa Japanese BBQ

CHAPTER ONE
THE BEGINNING

Whole-Ground Beef Concept

I T ALL STARTED on a day when I was driving back from the ranch. I was living a couple of towns away in a nice neighborhood with great schools. My father had recently passed away suddenly, and I found myself spending more and more time out on the ranch I grew up on. I somehow felt closer to him out there, where every inch of the property held memories to be treasured. In hindsight, I was feeling the pull back to the place where I grew up and was wanting to spend more and more of my time there despite the luxury and benefits I would be leaving behind.

When we lose someone close, we never want the memories to fade. And on this particular day, after being at the ranch and reminiscing on the days gone by, my thoughts drifted to the old days growing up when we had our dairy farm. We always had fresh milk in the refrigerator, and most of the time we had fresh beef in the freezer. A thought filtered into my mind, a question really, "People sell fresh milk, but why isn't anyone selling all-natural whole-ground beef like we enjoyed when I was a kid?" When we ran out of fresh ground beef, Mom would have to buy it at the store. I could smell the difference as it cooked in the pan. It did not smell fresh, and Mom would have to season the meat as soon as it started cooking to keep the house from smelling horrible. Our fresh ground beef smelled like a fine steak searing in a pan. I hated the taste and smell of grocery store ground beef.

I know that may sound like a wild and specific series of thoughts, but as I drove home that day, my mind raced from memory to memory, from home-cooked dinner to home-cooked dinner. I began to formulate a plan to offer the type of ground beef I grew up eating. The "Wells" concept began to take shape in my mind.

I had been researching the health benefits of grass-fed beef since having a personal health scare a couple of years prior to my father's passing. I was closely watching what I ate. Grass-fed beef is packed with health benefits. It was becoming more sought-after every day. My plan to offer a great tasting, top-quality ground beef that is also healthy was coming together! It was also interesting to discover that families consume several times the amount of ground beef as they do steaks or other cuts of beef. So, concentrating on whole-ground beef made sense.

To assure myself that I was not just emotional and missing my dad, I decided not to go public with my idea yet. We had a family vacation planned in the next few weeks, and I determined to wait to announce the idea upon returning home.

We had a great Colorado vacation. We trail-rode up the Colorado Rockies and saw the Great Divide from the high trail. I tried my hand at fly fishing and caught several amazing rainbow trout. But all the while, I was contemplating the "whole-ground beef" product launch.

My wife and I discussed many details of the launch privately as we navigated the roads to and from Colorado. She mainly listened to me talk about the plans and ideas as they would pop into my head. Ever since we were high school sweethearts, she has believed in me. The main thing I remember about that trip was that she never said a negative thing about my ideas. She somehow saw that what I was dreaming actually could happen. I will always appreciate her faith in my crazy ideas.

Upon returning home, I began the process of making this new concept available to the community. I went to my website developer, and we started the website. That same day, I had a Facebook page activated for the new Wells Cattle Co. concept. The page explained how I grew up with this amazing ground beef that would now be made available to the public. It was clean beef that was free of chemicals, medications, or hormones. It was the best hamburger meat anyone could ever enjoy because it included the entire side of beef, deboned and ground together: in other words, including the steaks and prime cuts, unlike other ground beef, which consists of extra fat and leftover meat trimmings. My first cow was sold before I could get it to the processor! The sales were done on my newly formed Facebook page. It was an exciting time as I brought this unique product to market.

As the word continued to spread that we were offering our prime whole-ground beef, there were plenty of naysayers. The old-time ranchers seemed to be the most critical of the idea. They could not imagine grinding up the ribeyes and filets into hamburger meat. But despite all of that, we grew steadily as more people heard about our unique product. Over the next year, we grew to become a good-sized local beef provider. Little did we know that the biggest opportunity was about to present itself.

Cheeseburger in Paradise
~ Jimmy Buffett

Our first butcher beef

Opportunities Have a Lifetime

AUTHOR AND SPEAKER Leonard Ravenhill said, "Opportunities of a lifetime must be seized within the lifetime of the opportunity." After providing our whole-ground beef through local pick-up and home delivery for several months, I decided to offer it to some local restaurant owners. After stopping by a few places, I realized that it would require more than just a regular scope of business to envision a restaurant concept using more expensive ground beef. As I followed up on samples I had delivered, the response was always the same. "Man, that has to be the best beef I have ever tasted, but I just don't see how I could make any money if I used it." The owners' traditional thinking robbed them of their opportunity to see an amazing burger being offered to their customers.

I remember saying to each of these owners that I believed there was a market in our area for a true ranch-raised premium burger, one made with the freshest ingredients and my whole-ground beef. But after several tries, I abandoned the idea of selling to restaurants, and we continued selling just to our local residential customer base.

Several months after the effort to offer our beef to restaurants, I received a phone call. The call started with a nice lady saying, "You probably don't remember me, but you dropped off some beef for us to sample a few months ago. We were not in a place to launch a new menu item." Then she gave me her name and the restaurant name, and I immediately remembered her!

Her restaurant was in an old 1930s home that had been converted into a restaurant in the heart of downtown Rockwall. I loved her place and will never forget the times my wife and I had eaten there. One time, as we were enjoying a Sunday lunch with our family there, I said to my wife, "I could see us owning this place if it ever comes up for sale."

As the phone conversation with the lady continued, she said, "My sister and I are considering retirement. I wanted to see if you would be interested in buying our restaurant and trying your burger concept here?" Oh, my! I could not believe the words I was hearing over the phone that day!

We had looked at another restaurant location rather seriously, but it was outside of town and had other types of businesses right up next to it sharing the same gravel parking lot. It really was not an ideal location we were learning, in a thriving city like Rockwall, Texas, retail space especially, for restaurants, does not become available very often.

So, when the lady made this offer, I was excited to speak with her. We met and came to an agreement on an amazing deal for their building and equipment. We allowed them to close on their own terms, and then we began remodeling. We were able to open within a few short weeks. We had generated so much excitement with our current beef customers that we had to sell tickets to our three-night soft-opening event. I will forever be grateful for our amazing location in downtown Rockwall, Texas. It was a blessing, but we were about to start a rapid learning curve about the good and bad of owning a restaurant.

I will admit this little fact now: I am glad I never started selling beef to local restaurants. Sometimes the answer "No" makes for a beautiful future, even when it does not feel great in the moment. I will always be thrilled to say that we seized a wonderful opportunity for our starting location! I will never regret taking the leap of faith when the opportunity presented itself to launch Wells Cattle Co. Burgers and Pies!

> *Opportunities of a lifetime must be seized*
> *within the lifetime of the opportunity.*
> *~ Leonard Ravenhill*

No Overnight Greatness

NOTHING GREAT HAPPENS overnight. As much as each of us would love for our efforts to be an instant success, they usually are not. The old saying is true. "Great things take time."

When we started in the restaurant business, our heart was in the right place. Our product concept was good. However, our execution had not been perfected. We had never operated a restaurant, and we were learning on the job in real time! We had a lot to learn! We had to develop our product offering and methods over time. It was several weeks before we really started seeing the 5-star reviews add up.

It seems that many people stop short of finding their greatness. Most things in life do not happen as quickly as we think they should. Although greatness is a journey that takes longer than we want it to, we must stay the course. One thing we had going for us was our pursuit of excellence. We may not have started out doing everything the best way, but we were not afraid to throw out a bad process when we learned of a better approach. One of our founding principles has been to remain teachable when there is something new to learn. We strive to work hard while remaining humble.

Recently, I watched the documentary *Jiro Dreams of Sushi,* where the story is told of the legendary Japanese sushi master, Jiro Ono. The film follows him for several days and tells of his life and amazing accomplishments. One of the statements that resonated with me was when he said that he was told as a boy that everything that could be done with sushi had been done. Now this man is 97 years old at the time of this writing, and he is still regarded by his peers as the best sushi chef ever to have lived. He refused to believe that the best had been accomplished. He said about being the greatest, "It's just about making an effort and repeating the same thing every day. It has to be better than the last time." There is a reason why great restaurants are great. It is no accident. It is not easy. But true greatness is inspiring and worth the daily effort.

In our pursuit of operating the best restaurant we possibly can, we have learned that everything can be improved in some way. To be the best we can be is simply a passion within our hearts. We constantly ask ourselves if there is a better product or a better process we can use to produce a better burger experience. One of the greatest business books of all time is *Good to Great* by Jim Collins. It is the only book I can remember reading cover to cover with a highlighter. The best line in the book is: "Good is the enemy of great." I love that line! If we settle for *good enough*, we will never experience the *greatness* that is just ahead.

I cannot tell you how many times I have sat down at a restaurant and felt that someone just threw something on a menu and never looked back. Worse yet is when they just throw something on the plate that is barely *good enough*. It is hardly edible when it is deemed *just good enough* in the kitchen. We cannot be afraid to push forward. We cannot be afraid to throw away a plate of food or even an entire bowl or tub. Why would we ever serve anything that we are not proud of?

As many inventors and engineers say when developing a new product or idea, "Do not be afraid to change or stop doing something that is not pushing towards excellence." We can fall into the trap of continuing to do something just because we have too much invested to stop. Elon Musk, one of our greatest modern minds, said in an interview, "One of the biggest traps we as engineers fall into is optimizing a thing that shouldn't exist." He was speaking about a product that has received so many features, man-hours, and design resources that one cannot afford to stop its production. This product develops a life and budget of its own, and so the engineers just keep trying to make it work. They cannot part with the beloved item now, and the item weighs the entire process down and results in failure. It is human nature not to give up on something you are heavily invested in; however, we must admit when things are not working and move on to better outcomes.

Can we apply this discussion to our world of small business or restaurants? How many menu items are not selling or perhaps not getting rave reviews? Why not cut them from the menu? Why not spend time and effort developing something new, exciting, and great rather than continuing the efforts to bring that good but not great idea along? You may discover the best thing you ever created was just beyond that tired old thing you have been working with for so long.

Greatness takes seasoning and time. It takes time to create tender, flavorful dishes, and the same is true with business. Keep evolving. Keep making incremental changes. Push past good and on toward greatness.

One of the most memorable things about Chef Jiro and his life of pushing for the greatest possible restaurant was the story of the octopus. Chef Jiro had already received the coveted three Michelin Stars, and with that great accomplishment, the "massage time" for their octopus was thirty minutes. That was the acceptable standard, an award-winning standard, until he discovered that forty-five minutes created true greatness. Can you imagine massaging octopus in a bowl for thirty minutes a day and then saying it can be even better? Then you increase that one task in a busy kitchen to forty-five minutes! "Good enough" will never allow you to achieve the level of "Great." To Chef Jiro, even the accomplishment of being a highly praised Michelin restaurant was not his mark of greatness. He never once considered halting his quest for true greatness. Never allow accolades from others to be a guide for your personal best. It is an amazing feeling to be recognized for the success you have achieved, but always stay hungry for the next level of greatness. Only you can discover what you can achieve! We cannot afford to simply settle for "good enough" when our customers deserve our very best!

Good is the enemy of Great.
~ Jim Collins

Our Ranch-Table Difference

ONE OF THE distinct differences that we offer is the amazing quality of our beef. As I have mentioned before, growing up, I was fortunate to experience the best ranch-raised beef anyone has ever eaten. We produce that same quality pasture-raised beef today, exclusively from our ranch.

We offer the highest quality of ground beef one can find, and we call it "whole-ground beef." This means we include every cut of beef in the grind. That's right! All steaks, loin, briskets, roasts . . . ALL IN! We believe this makes the very best hamburger anyone has ever tasted.

While many have decided to offer specific USDA-certified programs, we chose to stay away from the "certified labels" and simply say "pasture-raised" instead. This better describes our process and procedure. Our cattle are raised in an open-pasture environment. We do not use growth hormones, growth antibiotics, or grain-based diets. However, we use high protein supplements as a high-fat boost in cold winter months when grass is out of season and hay may not be enough to sustain the needs of our premium cattle. We do not feel like this harms the cattle or the meat but is beneficial to the overall health of the animals.

Many beef providers try to use the term "grass-fed" to differentiate their products from others, but in my opinion, the term is over-used and abused by many in our day. Well-meaning people use this term to market cattle and beef without understanding the strict USDA guidelines. Much of the beef sold under the label "grass-fed" might be finished in the final weeks and months on grain to accelerate growth and profits. There are so many caveats and loopholes with what "grass-fed" means, we choose not to use the term in our company. We strive to be honest and lead our business with the utmost integrity. Rather than playing games with government certifications and labels, we simply tell you what we do! Life is simpler when people are clear with their processes and product offerings. No games. Just honest beef.

Our goal is to provide the best possible beef to our customers. This means clean, healthy, fat, strong cattle. No growth hormones are used and no grain rations. We grass-finish each animal we process. This provides a clean diet for the proper cleansing of any toxins that could affect the meat. If we source local animals from surrounding farms, we can be sure the final days before processing are clean, healthy, and to our highest standards. We provide lush grasses and quality hay for our cattle to provide the most premium beef possible.

We use a local beef processor that is overseen by state-certified inspectors. Animals are inspected both on the hoof and once on the rail. Our beef is then subject to sample testing by state inspectors. To ensure our high-quality standards are met, one of our employees is allowed to accompany our animals through the entire butchering process. Over the years, we have been involved in this process and maintain full confidence in the quality service our processor provides.

All these points result in a superior product over anything bought in a store or provided by a wholesale meat company. There is simply no comparison to our quality assurance program from the ranch to the table.

To further this discussion on superior beef, there are several differences we see when it comes to local ranchers. Here are a few:

Local ranchers care about their animals and their reputation. The quality of beef speaks these truths loud and clear. From their pastures, feeds, hay production, and vaccination choices, everything they do is to produce the best animals they can for the customer.

Local ranchers are not mass feedlots. Many feedlots house an average of one hundred head of cattle per acre of land and are forced to use prescription medications just to keep their animals alive. Some antibiotics are mixed directly into their feed at regular intervals because cattle are kept in such close quarters that they cannot create enough space to remain healthy. This close contact always allows for infection to spread quickly from pen to pen.

Local ranchers are running smaller operations and can keep up with their stock and handpick those animals that are ready for processing. They do not use a computer program or a predetermined timeline. If an animal is not ready to go, the rancher waits and continues to invest in that animal until the time is right.

Local ranchers are not getting wealthy by selling beef. It is a labor of love and gives a sense of pride to be able to help families in a way that blesses their dinner table. Farming and ranching are not big money-making operations; for the most part, they are barely self-sustaining. Large processing companies receive government subsidies that offset their operational costs. I do not personally know of one local rancher who receives any of these types of government payouts to offset their feed costs or acquisition costs. The numbers we work within are true figures. It is said that a rancher is the only entity that has to buy everything at retail price and sell everything at wholesale price.

Local ranchers that I know are honest, hard-working, and giving people. The old saying, "Give you the shirt off their backs" probably came from a rancher. They are just good folks. And I know a lot of them!

I will close by saying this. Local ranchers are not going to process sick cattle, cancer cattle, drugged-up cattle, or crippled cattle. They cannot! The local processors will not take them. They must be healthy or local guys will not process them. This is not the case for chain stores and wholesale meat processors. They allow the most atrocious animals onto their kill floor. There is literally no standard too low for them to be deemed usable.

Local meat should be the highest quality meat you can put on your table. It is better than most restaurants' meat bought from mass wholesalers and better than grocery stores' meat. Our beef is absolutely the best because our reputation depends upon it. I love to see people support local farms and ranches. This support enables those families to continue doing what they love for their community!

I would rather be on my farm than be emperor of the world!
~ George Washington

Our Menu Strategy

ONE OF THE other major areas where we have pushed ourselves to be great is our menu. When we first began, we simply served our Wells beef burgers, a pasture-raised chicken burger, and a Wells beef bratwurst, along with fresh-cut fries and a salad. We had a few desserts, but overall, a very simple menu. As we gained more knowledge of how the burger business worked, I sat down one day and created a "burger list" that named burgers and listed the various ingredients they would contain. This is a story all in itself. I did not realize many chefs tasted their food before adding it to the menu. I just sat down one night after a long day and started creating burger ideas on my laptop. There was the Western Burger with cheddar, crispy bacon, grilled onions, jalapeños, and house-made barbeque sauce. That sounded good. Then I added the Mushroom Swiss that was a regular on other restaurant menus with grilled mushrooms, grilled onions, Swiss cheese, and mayonnaise.

Then some crazy ideas started coming to mind. How about a German Burger with sauerkraut, grilled onions, crispy bacon, Swiss cheese, and spicy mustard? The list grew to twelve burgers, ending up with an outrageous Brunch Burger that is built on toasted waffles with pancake syrup drizzled on the cooked beef patty to which we added cheddar cheese and crispy bacon dressed with our house-made peanut butter sauce and then topped off with an egg fried according to the customer's preference.

We began to see excitement around the menu. All those creations could have been custom ordered at any time with our add-on style menu, but no one was thinking like that. So, the "burger list" catapulted us forward into a new era. Now people began to say things like, "We have to come back and try all of these burgers. They all sound so good!" Several times we heard, "I intend to try every burger. I'm going to eat my way down the list."

The next iteration of our menu added daily specials on Monday, Tuesday, and Wednesday to boost interest on our slower days of the week. These were marketing opportunities and drivers to encourage people to want to be with us on those days that were not as busy as the weekend. We tried several other special items in our first few years. Some were very successful for a while, and some were not. But we continued to learn and grow toward greatness.

One of the most extensive changes we made to our menu came when the price uptick began to hit home. You know, the one where inflation caused everyone to increase menu prices to stay open. We revamped our menu structure and revisited every item we offered. We removed some items and even added new ones. But everything we did was because it was a good decision for us as well as the customer. The biggest addition in our history came when we added our Wagyu beef hot dogs! We are the only restaurant in town to offer farm-to-table Wagyu hot dogs. We did it correctly from the first day we sold them, blending them seamlessly into our existing menu choices. We not only had a Burger List that named our burgers and their toppings, but we offered a Hot Dog List as well, with plenty of choices and options. Now our topping combinations range from a standard backyard dog to Chicago-style, and we even have a few dogs topped with a fried egg. Then the hot dog toppings go into the realm of crazy-good! We have one dog with our house-made peanut butter sauce, grape jelly, roasted hatch green chiles, and crispy bacon!

The latest big change we have made is the addition of hand-dipped ice cream shakes. Our shakes are made from the same ice cream we serve on top of some of our desserts. It comes from a local creamery up the road. We offer the three standard flavors: chocolate, strawberry, and vanilla. They can be served along with meals or afterward for dessert.

We have been slow to change, but ready when the time was right to move toward a better product offering and menu. We have not been afraid to add or take away items, but we also do not make changes merely for the sake of change. Every move we have made has been strategically advantageous for us and, we believe, for our customers. We are not overly attached to anything except our core menu offerings, which are our reason for existing. We have pushed for the greatest menu possible.

We now have an extensive gluten-free menu that offers a bakery fresh gluten-free bun, a dedicated fryer, and several different house-made desserts. We also have the largest keto-friendly and diabetic-friendly menu around, and we offer more safety measures for all dietary allergens than any restaurant we know.

Offering specialty menu items is not enough if the kitchen process is not protecting the food as it moves through the line. Our processes include changing gloves and utilizing dedicated cutting boards and bun toasters to guard against cross-contamination. We have chosen to keep our fryer dedicated to non-gluten items for our hand-cut fries and other fried menu offerings. However, that prohibits us from offering items like battered onion rings and fried pickles due to the cross-contamination of the oil. We are honored to be trusted with the health and wellness of our customers, and why not? Our customers deserve the very best!

We have continued to keep excitement going with our menu since our opening. We have made a few strategic changes, but we remain faithful to what has gotten us this far. If you notice, successful restaurants like Chick-fil-A keep a standard menu, making only small changes over the years. They would never remove their core concept, The Original Chicken Sandwich. Likewise, Wells will never eliminate its core concept, The Wells Beef Burger.

Many times, a marker of a fledgling restaurant or franchise is the many menu changes. This can be detrimental to the diner's experience. It is frustrating to order entrees that you enjoy and then return to see them replaced with something new for no apparent reason. There is comfort in knowing the customer can count on finding those beloved menu items he or she has been craving. Those favorites may be what brings them back for a repeat visit. Sometimes the menu changes so often that the waitstaff cannot keep up. There have been times when they have had to ask to see the customer's menu to answer a question when attempting to take the order. That is simply too much change!

It is understandable for restaurants to offer specials on certain days of the week or even have a changing menu slot every month or so, but to change the menu randomly without cause or warning is a bad business practice, in my opinion. My family frequents a couple of different taco shops in our city that have fun monthly or weekly taco creations, but these are always in addition to the standard menu they have had for years. Menu consistency is key to building trust with the customer base.

One final thought about our menu offerings is our commitment to the kiddos. Since our first day, we have viewed our "Kids Zone Menu" to be as important as anything else we offer. We picked items that would resonate with their tastebuds, like the Wells beef burger slider, wagyu hotdog, grilled cheese on a slider bun, and a kid favorite, the grilled PBJ! All come with fries, a drink, and a bag of fruit snacks for less money than a single third-pound burger. We wanted our restaurant to be affordable for families with children. Being parents of two girls who traveled everywhere with us, we were always disappointed when a restaurant did not consider the needs of our children.

We have an extremely successful rapport with our young customers. They love our food and the fruit snacks, too. Their parents appreciate that we offer affordable meals for their children. We also have a great "clean plate" average going. I believe kids know the difference between real food from a farm and boxed meals and fast food from a drive-thru. We hear about it almost every day when parents say, "My kid never eats all of his food, but he cleans his plate here!" At Wells we consider that one of the highest compliments.

I don't want to hear the specials. If they're
so special, put 'em on the menu.
~ Jerry Seinfeld

Making Big Decisions

SOME DECISIONS HAVE the power to make your future, while others can absolutely destroy your business. Every decision must be weighed and calculated by the most important criteria in your life for the results to benefit you long-term. We have made some great decisions, and we have made some that did not work out as well. In the end, these questions must be answered: are you ready for this opportunity, and can you handle this change right now? Even if something sounds amazing, you still must be able to function as you move forward.

Chris was one of our very first customers. I will never forget his first visit. He went on and on about the quality of our food. He just kept saying, "Man, I don't think you know what you have here." Later I found out that Chris was part owner in several restaurants in Dallas, and now he owns two very successful restaurants himself. He told me that he wanted to be our first franchise, and I may hold him to that someday if we ever decide to go in that direction. Chris became a regular. Then one day he said, "I have a guy you need to meet." I agreed because he often brought groups of people in to show them what a Wells burger was all about. This was a big day because he brought in Brian, one of the biggest names in the food and beverage industry, to meet me and enjoy a Wells burger.

Brian came in and was an instant fan of our food from his first visit. He had very nice things to say about the quality of the food and the laid-back country vibe. Then he said something I was not expecting. He said, "I have a client that wants a Wells in their upcoming project." To be honest, by now I had heard this several times, so I accepted the compliment and moved on. Then he got more serious. He said they had secret-shopped our restaurant twice with two different teams, and the unanimous consensus was that they want to recreate this place down to the materials used to build it originally.

I thought, "This is crazy; this building was built in the thirties, almost one hundred years ago!" Again, I thanked him for his kindness and asked out of curiosity, "Where is this place being built?" He said, "A town all the way across the Dallas-Fort Worth Metroplex." I popped off and said, "It would take a helicopter to get me out there!" and we both laughed.

Two days later, I received a call from Brian, and he told me that he had my helicopter. He asked if I could make it to Love Field Private Side the next Wednesday morning at ten o'clock. Well, there went all my excuses! So, off I went the next Wednesday morning, walking out onto the tarmac to board a Bell Jet helicopter! This country boy from rural America getting to fly first class across Dallas was most definitely a "cool" experience. I hesitate to name-drop because as nice as those people were, it just did not seem feasible for me to say "Yes." They are a big-name firm with billions of dollars to invest in real estate and ideas they believe in. Even though I turned down their offer, they did have WELLS on the plat, and we were center development just as they had promised. They were ready to bring in their architects to begin discussions on raw materials, kitchen size, and indoor and outdoor dining layouts. They were committed to seeing us as part of their plan.

I will always be honored, but it just was not the right time. I could not see myself on the road every day to their side of the Metroplex with two teenage daughters at home and a young restaurant to navigate. The timing to jump into that opportunity did not seem right. They were gracious in accepting my decision to decline their amazing offer. But I stand today proud of my decision. We have continued to grow and learn more about the industry, and we are better today than ever. I am not sure we could have done as well being spread that thin, especially with the then-coming disaster of Covid and the challenges those ensuing months brought. Brian is still my friend, and we meet to discuss opportunities whenever they arise, and Chris still comes in and enjoys our food as much today as he did in the beginning!

Decisions are important and can be the greatest of opportunities or the most detrimental of choices. We must keep the most important parts of our life close during those decision-making times. Staying true to family, faith, and those existing commitments we have is of the utmost importance! We cannot afford to lose out on what is most important to who we are.

You are only one decision from a totally different life.
~ Wilfred Peterson

Inspiration to Dream

WHEN YOU WALK into our restaurant, you may notice the cast iron cow on the counter. About one year before opening our restaurant in downtown Rockwall, Texas, my wife and I visited Pawhuska, Oklahoma. We toured the studio of the Food Network's Pioneer Woman - Ree Drummond. We visited the Drummond Ranch and shopped in The Pioneer Woman Mercantile. My wife bought a few items, and I carried around a small cast iron cow that had caught my eye. When Lynda asked, "What did you find to buy?" I showed her the cow I had picked up. Her curiosity was obvious when she asked, "What made you pick that cow up?"

I simply said, "One day this will sit on the counter of our restaurant we will open."

She simply said, "Okay," and that was that. In hindsight, she may not have thought I was being serious, or maybe she did not quite hear me. But nothing more was said about it. I bought it and brought it home to sit on a shelf until it could find its rightful place on that future counter.

My inspiration for the cow was two-fold that day. First, my dad had been a ranch foreman on the neighboring Chapman-Barnard Ranch. At that time, the ranch was the largest in Oklahoma, with 85,000 acres! That was in the 1960s and was before my time. But the stories of that old time still ring in my ears. I grew up hearing tales of the ranch life just outside of Pawhuska, and to go back to that area as an adult was sentimental and special. It was a trip that spurred my imagination to think back over those days gone by as we drove across the Northern Oklahoma prairie. Dad spoke often of his days riding saddle bronc and bareback, training horses, working cattle, including a couple of near-death experiences, all of them as true as the bluestem prairie and Oklahoma blue sky.

My second inspiration for that cast iron cow comes from my time spent around the Pioneer Woman's facilities that weekend. I was in awe of the excellence of the construction, organization, and quality of one woman's dream. The food was outstanding; the buildings were immaculate, and most inspiring was that she saw this dream before it was ever built. She saw something in the streets of her tired old downtown. She somehow saw people coming from all around to experience her vision, her unique take on life, and the amazing food she prepared.

As I walked around the Mercantile that weekend, I said to myself, "If she can build this here, I can build a restaurant in Rockwall. I can serve a different burger with the highest quality whole-ground beef, and people will come." That may sound farfetched, but that little cast iron cow was a seed of someone else's doing what others may have doubted, to create what others could not yet see.

Today we are just over five years old. We have built additional back seating that doubled our original capacity; we have found a way to double our kitchen space and have even added extra parking. We have streamlined processes to be able to meet the demand of any rush hour we have experienced so far.

We began in a small house that barely seated forty people. We washed and painted the old 1930s downtown house, created a unique environment both inside and out, and paid a ton of money to keep the old equipment working. Now each morning, as we turn on the open signs, the cast iron cow is in its place on the desk to watch the dream become reality.

I was told by several close friends and even local business owners not to open in our current location. They said things like, "That building has never been very successful, and nothing else has ever stayed open very long there." I had one person tell me that we would never make it there! But I could see it. Somehow, I knew if it was operated with excellence, served with top quality and genuine hospitality, it would work. And we have managed to exceed everyone's highest expectations, even our own!

It is the inspirations we find along the way that fuel our desire to inspire someone else one day. I often think back on our weekend trip to Pawhuska. I am thankful I felt the challenge to go home and create something that had never been done before. In a similar way, I feel this book may be a small inspiration to help someone else along the way. Just because everyone else may not see what you see does not mean it cannot exist someday, especially if you vow to do it right!

The only thing that is worse than being
blind is having sight but no vision.
~ Helen Keller

The Cast-iron Cow

CHAPTER TWO
CULINARY FOUNDATIONS

After School Special

D AD OWNED AN old set of mounted longhorns long before he and Mom were married. He loved those old things. The story goes that, when they first were wed, he had the longhorns proudly displayed in the living room. But it was not long before they were demoted to the back room of the house, an old, converted garage they called their den. I remember from my childhood that they were eventually relegated to the garage in the house we now call the bunkhouse on the ranch. Several years ago, as an adult, I remodeled the living room for Mom and Dad. I removed the hayloft floor from our old barn and used that wood for wainscoting around the bottom of the wall and around the fireplace. Then, without asking Mom for permission, Dad and I placed the old longhorns right over the fireplace and under the bright focus of a three-light track that I installed to highlight the old horns. Once Mom saw them in place, she was finally in love with them and mentioned several times how they had become her favorite part of the room. Now when you come into our restaurant to order, look up at the wall. Mounted just above the double windows is that same set of longhorns. What was once a point of contention is now a focal point of daily celebrations. The same is true with my after-school search for something to eat.

After school, I was always hungry and ready for a snack. My father worked on the ranch and would come in around dark, and my mother taught school an hour away. This left my brother and me to find our own after-school snack. Many times, this took some creativity. If my memory serves me correctly, we did not have much available to eat. Mom and Dad never bought snack foods. But we always seemed to have potatoes in the pantry, so for years, I would come home and microwave a potato. I would then create a butter sauce to spice up the plain baked potato.

I would start with salted butter and then add a little more salt and pepper, but then the experimentation would begin. I probably tried every seasoning in the pantry and many in combination with others. Without realizing it, I began to learn each ingredient's flavor profile and how it blended with others. Little did I know this phase of my life would teach my palette things some people never learn. There are some amazing flavors that work well together, and then there are some spices that should never be seen in the same dish at the same time.

Today I can usually identify flavors and spices within food with ease. It also makes recipe development much easier with this foundation I learned without even realizing it in my after-school self-taught culinary class.

Many years ago, I fell in love with a spice blend I had in a restaurant on a steak. I tried to buy it and even tried to find a recipe for the blend, but I eventually gave up on that idea and began to figure out my own recipe. After several tries, I was able to get it to taste really close to what I remembered the original flavor being. I then began to use it on my steaks and burgers at home. As you might guess, when we opened the restaurant, this became our signature seasoning for our burgers!

I have since created all five of the sauces that we make regularly in our restaurant. We have some basic sauces that we purchase, but even some of the standard ones contain a unique, flavorful twist. We make our own blend of spicy ketchup, jalapeño ranch, barbeque sauce, New Mexico red chile sauce, and even a creamy peanut butter sauce! We are asked all the time to bottle every sauce we make. Who knew how useful my after-school potato butter-making skills would be someday?

Like those old longhorns that were once a point of frustration are now a priceless part of our rustic atmosphere. I feel the same way about my early discovery of seasonings and spices. As a kid, I would have loved more store-bought snacks, but now I would not trade my experience for anything. It is a priceless part of who I am.

Good food is very often simple food.
~ Anthony Bourdain

Sauce Is Boss

WE NEED FLAVORS that appeal to the greatest number of customers possible. We will never please everyone, but that should not mean we are not pleasing a very large number of people every day!

Several weeks after opening the restaurant, an idea came to me, "We need spicy ketchup!" It was on a morning drive into the restaurant when this thought hit me. As I pondered the idea, the recipe ingredients began to come to me. The recipe would obviously begin with a base of Heinz ketchup, and then we would need pickled jalapeños along with some of their juice. My thoughts continued until I arrived at the restaurant. By the time I stepped out of the truck, I had ninety percent of the recipe completed in my head.

Once in the kitchen, I went straight to the Vitamix, and the process began: measuring, tasting, and making notes. It was easy sailing until the final tasting. Something was lacking.

The sauce needed to be brightened up. It hit me. I knew what to add. It started with just a tablespoon and then two. To this day, we still do not share that final ingredient with those who ask. It is a secret. Many have guessed, but none have guessed correctly. I slid the note card over to my kitchen manager and said: "That's our new Wells Spicy Ketchup recipe!" We have never touched that recipe blend since. I estimate that we now serve roughly thirty-five to forty gallons of spicy ketchup a month, and it has become a staple of our house-made complementary sauces. Our customers love our sauces and often request that we bottle them.

Many chefs pride themselves on "their food" and do not consider the customer as they should. And I get it! It takes confidence to create a dish and then serve it to others, but ultimately, we are catering to the greatest number of paying customers we can fit into our facility at service times. While we are not all about simply making money, we must be profitable enough to reopen again next month and the next, and so on.

Recently I was watching a food competition show. The guy who lost responded, "But at least I did my thing. I fed them my food, and I'm proud of that." On the other hand, the guy who won said, "I paid attention to what the judges enjoyed and tried my best to make dishes that pleased their palettes." Just as these two contestants found out, one wins, and one almost wins. An interesting side note about the show contestants: the winning chef was a home chef with no formal training, while the second-place chef had many years of training at Michelin Star restaurants and even sat under a James Beard award-winning chef. Experience does not always result in good flavor and wide appeal.

It does not matter how much you like your own flavor preferences; you must listen to the overarching sound of the customer if you want to be the winner of their business. With that said, there are always folks who would not know good flavor if it was poured into their mouth. So, use wisdom to determine which voices to hear and which to ignore. I have a good friend who tried our fresh ground beef, and he said he preferred the taste of regular Walmart meat. To each his own, I guess.

I was on a vacation to Middle America a couple of years ago, and we picked a nice place for dinner that was close to the hotel where we were staying. We noticed the ratings were solid, but not great, maybe around three stars, but we did not want to travel too far that night in the cold. As we walked in, we noticed the trendy décor, and we observed there was no wait for our table even though it was dinner time. We noticed the empty tables as we progressed through the dining room, but we were there, so we tried to make the best of the night.

We all ordered similar dishes, and as we began to taste our steak, I noticed an unusual flavor that I was not accustomed to. Then my wife said something about a different flavor on her steak. The room was dimly lit, so it was hard to make out every detail of the skillet-style plate we were eating from. We then tasted the whipped potatoes and found another strange flavor. Now we were all guessing what these flavors were. They were not bad, but they were different and somewhat unpleasant. As our discussion continued, we all came up with our own ideas as to what the chef had done to our food. When the waiter returned, we asked for clarification to see who was closest to the flavors' identities. You may love these flavors, but the steak was sitting in a bitter-orange citrus sauce, and the potatoes were whipped with malt vinegar powder. Creative maybe but not "blowing the doors off the place" delicious.

That chef was doing his own thing. He did *his* flavors without regard for the *consumer's* palette. He was doing *his* thing, but almost by himself. That is not a successful restaurant plan, and it is certainly not a sensible menu plan. When we can give the customers what they want, we should strive to do so. After all, the customers are choosing to spend their money where they want, and we are privileged when they spend it at our business.

A final thought on sauce and flavor. Flavor must be balanced toward the entire meal. Have you been to a restaurant that serves a set number of courses? Perhaps a five-course meal? The meal will begin with a light, small plate, somewhat on the bland side of the flavor spectrum. Then perhaps a light soup, maybe a seasonal squash base, or a clear broth-style recipe. But with each course, more flavor is introduced until the main dish is seasoned perfectly, and you can taste the intricacies of the chef's specialty.

In contrast, have you ever been to a restaurant where everything you order is super flavorful? I remember a recent visit to a local barbeque restaurant. I love Texas barbeque! But what I noticed was the habanero mac and cheese had a ton of flavor and a kick of heat. Plus, the beans were delicious with another kick of their own salty jalapeño heat. Then the bark on the brisket was powerfully salty, black peppery, and sweet. By the time I had taken one bite of each item on my plate, my palette was blown out. Everything was great by itself, but not balanced for an entire meal.

As chefs, it is our responsibility to balance flavors to endure through the entire meal. Could we add more spice to this item or that course of a meal? Sure. But how will that extra spice and flavor multiply more and more as it is eaten? Many times, we cannot tell the total palette picture in just one bite or one spoonful. The greatest chefs among us know how to balance flavors, spices, rubs, and sauces for the entire dining experience. The "greats" among us know how to orchestrate each seasoning and spice as a symphony to be enjoyed over an evening rather than in just a few initial palette-blinding bites.

With any menu item we have implemented, we have started by asking our kitchen team to sample and give feedback. We also ask several customers to try the item. Finally, we watch the response over the next several weeks for true customer acceptance. If it is not a customer favorite, we must go back to the cutting board and create something they love. I am happy that so many people love the flavors on our menu and the house-made spicy ketchup!

> *Hunger is the best sauce in the world.*
> *~ Miguel de Cervantes*

All Five Senses

AS A LOVER of restaurants all my life, I have studied my experiences across all types of eateries, from family-owned local spots to the finest dining establishments across the nation. I have seen some things that were amazing and some things that were extremely unfortunate in relation to how our senses process our dining experience. What I have seen is that the best restaurants pay attention to each of the five senses. Yes, all five! So many restaurants focus on staying open that they forget every customer walks in with their senses ready to interpret their dining experience.

To begin, we know *taste* is the obvious focus on most people's minds, but each of our five senses is tied to our other senses. Our sense of smell is closely tied to our sense of taste. Therefore, if a restaurant smells like sewer gas, the odor will ruin the dining experience. There is power in a pleasant smell. When I visited Las Vegas recently, I learned that casinos pump fragrances into their air-handling systems to create an enhanced environment and excite the senses as you walk into their property. Another example is the way many people associate an enjoyable time at the movies with the powerful fragrance of buttered popcorn. You may have noticed when walking into a Buc-ee's for fuel or a restroom stop that the smell of cinnamon is always in the air. Part of their tradition is to keep pecans roasting in sugary cinnamon butter to create that inviting aroma wafting through the air as you arrive. It is a delicious welcome every time!

Several years ago, we were selling our home, and the real estate agent arrived for an open house event carrying a batch of cookie dough. She saw me notice the package of dough and said, "I'll pop these in the oven for a few minutes and make your house smell like a home!" She knew that there would be an instant connection to memories of home with just the scent of freshly baked cookies in the air that connects people back to their childhood. Our sense of smell should never be overlooked in the restaurant industry.

Just as important as our sense of *smell* is our eyesight. It has been said that we eat with our eyes first. We see this idea on display in fine dining entrees. The plate is masterfully built with picturesque servings and sometimes even decorative drizzles to excite our palate with the beauty of the food before we ever taste the first bite.

On the other side of the spectrum, have you ever ordered from a picture on a menu, and then the food comes out looking like a Pinterest fail? It is hard to enjoy that dish when it does not even come close to what it is expected to look like. Appearance is extremely important, not only on the plate but also in the dining room, waiting areas, and especially the restrooms. All these areas help to create the overall ambiance of the establishment. People simply cannot ignore what they see, so we must make it a priority that they see beauty, cleanliness, and appetizing food.

Touch or feel is a sense we do not always automatically think of in the restaurant business. Yep! How does your table feel under your arms or hands? Is the clear coat breaking down to a sticky putty, gluing you to it with every touch? When you slide into a booth, is it cracking like a dead alligator's hide picking at your lady's pantyhose?

What about the mouthfeel? One of the most painstaking processes we have in our kitchen is preparing our 5.5-ounce whole-ground beef patties. We weigh each one and then form it using a 5-inch metal ring. Why do we do this when our beef processor would love to patty all that meat for us with their high-dollar machine? Because a hand-formed patty is tender! The machine-forming process ruins the mouth feel of the patty because it densely packs the meat together. We work hard to provide a patty with a true homemade texture. I believe the hand-forming of our beef directly affects the taste, texture, and uniqueness of our burgers.

Finally, our *hearing.* I believe our sense of hearing is the most underrated sense in the restaurant business, but it really is a powerful sense. It can be an overpowering sense. On our recent trip to Vegas, my wife and I decided to try one of the crazy, over-the-top shakes that are all the rage. You know, the ones that cost about twenty dollars and are larger than life! The kind with more candy and cookies stacked on top of the glass than shake inside the glass. We knew of just the spot in the area, and we walked up to ask for a quick table. We took the first one available without realizing it was right across the walkway from a construction zone. Evidently, they were jackhammering old concrete or something horrendous on the other side of the temporary sheetrock wall. It was ridiculous. I am not sure I could even taste the ice cream for the racket!

Hearing can impact our taste buds and affect our dining experience negatively. What we hear *is* important. How about the last time you were seated in a dining room next to a pair of screaming twins or that rambunctious little league baseball team? The noise you are forced to hear can seriously affect the overall enjoyment of your meal.

I am a sucker for nostalgia. We play nineties country music at our place, but not from a random playlist. Our playlist is curated with upbeat and positive songs. Sunshine, parties, and good times are a few of the themes of the songs we have playing. I think what we hear makes a difference. It can bring back the old days or a simpler time, and why not let those memories and emotions be associated with the dining experience?

We publish our Apple Music Playlist about once a year for our customers to download and listen to. I believe I have also heard our playlist while eating in at least three different restaurants in our area. You may say, "That is impossible to know. Those are hit songs, and anyone could use them." Very true; however, I listen to our playlist enough to know when I hear three or four songs in a row that match our playlist order. Regardless, it is an honor that others like our choice of music enough to use it as well! We take it as a compliment.

It matters what sounds we present. One wintry day, we chose to open when most restaurants were closed due to a snowstorm. I had several people ask specifically about our music because songs of summer and beaches stood out that day as a welcomed thought.

Remember for a moment the joy of sitting in your favorite Mexican restaurant, hungry and steadily trying to eat your weight in crispy tortilla chips while drowning your sorrows with a bowl of fresh salsa. Then you begin to hear the beautiful sound of sizzling fajitas coming through the restaurant. As they get closer, your eyes pick up on the deep green and rich red of the bell peppers. Then as they set the piping hot platter in front of you, you begin to feel the warmth of the skillet as they warn you it is a very hot plate. Then the smell of the rich smoky char makes your mouth water as you anticipate the delicious dinner you are about to enjoy.

Finally, you get the opportunity to put all your favorite ingredients into that warm tortilla as your taste buds have been primed by your four other senses! All four have participated to set the stage for your first bite. The flavor enhanced by all your senses being awakened by this culinary cocktail is genius. There is nothing like all five senses firing off together to complete a perfect first bite. I can almost taste it now!

The senses, being explorers of the world,
open the way to knowledge.
~ Maria Montessori

Wells Cattle Co. Burgers & Pies, Rockwall, TX

CHAPTER THREE
CUSTOMER CONNECTION

CHAPTER THREE

CUSTOMER CONNECTION

Tangible Touches

WHETHER IT IS a friendly handshake, a compassionate embrace, or a passing pat on the back, touch is well accepted and a powerful positive human connection. We see this power of touch at work when a horse clinician begins a training session with a new animal. The power of touch is the most powerful tool he or she has to communicate their intent to the animal. It is said that a horse can hear a heartbeat from up to four feet away, and he uses that perception to help gauge interaction. So, a horse really can sense the nerves or calm of a rider sitting on his back. It has always intrigued me to see the way different horses react to different people. Some people have a calming effect, while others seem to make the horse jumpy and even unpredictable at times.

About a year ago, we purchased an untrained three-year-old mare, a beautiful red roan from the Peppy San Badger line, and she was wild. We wanted to get her bred, and we knew she had to be gentle enough to load in and out of a trailer. She needed to be halter-broke to lead and calm enough to go to someone else's pasture. The first step was getting close enough to put a hand on her, an accomplishment that would take several days due to the amount of spunk she possessed. After a few days of working with her, she began to allow me to place the halter on her head and lead her around. It took a few more days to get her to load into a trailer, and then unloading was always an adventure. It seemed that she grew wings and flew out of the trailer. You just had to be ready to give her space to fly!

All the while, a gentle tone and touch were the tools that worked the very best. After her vacation at the breeder's place for a few weeks, the real test came the day we visited the veterinarian. That was a memorable day for both of us. She had to unload from the trailer and then be led into a new barn she had never seen before. Next, I led her into the inside of a building and then into a stall! This was an amazing feat for this young horse that had never been ridden or trained outside of the time we spent leading, but with that same gentle tone and calm touch, she followed my leading perfectly.

When people come into our business, we try to convey this same calm. We are always blessed when they choose us. I try to shake every hand I can to communicate our grateful heartbeat.

One time, I was in a training seminar, and the gentleman presenting was making the point that human touch is powerful and even electric in nature. I do not recall the university study he spoke about, but I will never forget the illustration he performed. He asked for a couple of volunteers to come up on stage with him, and he then asked them to hold hands while one held a children's light-up tennis shoe in the other hand. Next, he used an electric shock ring to give a small charge to the open hand of the other person. When he did this, the shoe lit up. The current moved from the farthest arm, through the connected hands, and out to the shoe which had been set on the far hand!

Then it got crazy! He asked the couple to let go of each other's hand and stand with their shoulders a couple of inches apart. He then sent the current again. Even with an air gap, the shoe lights lit up. He was proving that we all have an "electrical field" that we emit from our bodies. We know that our nervous system operates with electric pulses, as do our brain and heart. Could it be that when we reach out and connect with someone, part of our energy can be transmitted to them? I am not sure how far to take this discussion in this book, but I am a firm believer that, when we extend our hand to a guest, we connect our gratitude and our welcoming energy to them. We somehow communicate our heart's gratefulness with our human touch. We are thankful that they chose our restaurant, our food, and our family today.

While touch is an important part of our focus, so is verbal communication. When you sit down inside our restaurant, you will notice there are no televisions on the wall. This is by design. I do not have an issue with restaurants having screens; I have three menu screens in my ordering area. But I love conversation! It has always bothered me to sit across from someone in a restaurant just to have them look above my head for the entire meal while they watch whatever is on the screen behind me. We do play music in our dining rooms, but we hope it is never too loud to speak above to have a conversation. There are sports bars and wing joints that have their walls lined with screens for every sport in the world. However, at our place, we treasure conversation and the lack of chaos that all those screens bring.

I am sure there are many other studies available to read about. However, my philosophy has been to smile when I can, shake a hand when I can, pat a back when I can, and speak when I can. These methods of communication help convey the true feelings of the heart.

> *I've learned that people will forget what you*
> *said, people will forget what you did, but people*
> *will never forget how you made them feel.*
> ~ *Maya Angelou*

In Plain Sight

ONE OF THE primary goals at our restaurant is for our customers to feel as if they are having a burger out at the Wells Ranch. While that may sound silly, we hear this exact phrase and sentiment expressed by customers often! Being operated by family and those who act like family is very important, but that is not always enough. The owner's presence and visibility enrich the culture of hospitality.

There is a restaurant that we enjoy going to that is owned by a legendary Dallas-area restaurateur. Dale Wamstad (Del Frisco) has built some of the greatest brands in fine-dining steakhouses in Dallas, Texas. When we walk into his restaurant, we always know we are going to enjoy a great meal with great service. But there is something special about looking up and seeing him walk across the dining room. There is a reassurance in the air that everything is going to be par excellence. There seems to be a big difference between owning a business and showing ownership of that business. Dale has always encouraged the best in his staff and communicated that confidence to his customers. There is something powerful about the owner being present.

There are probably businesses where you know the owner and have had a chance to see him or her in their business or around town. And then, in contrast, there are other businesses, and probably most businesses we know, where we have never seen any evidence of ownership in or outside of their place of business. Many times, we would not even know how to contact the owner if we wanted to. One of our keys to success has been my accessibility and availability as the owner. I am not saying I hand out my personal phone number to everyone who walks in the door, but I am accessible via several different methods. Anyone can reach me at any of the social media direct messages or email at any time. But this discussion goes beyond those methods of connection. It is more about the principle of visibility than simply contacting me personally.

When we first began our beef business, I started a private Facebook group for our customers and those who wanted to keep an open communication with us. This avenue of communication has continued over the years. We have a great group of followers who receive notifications about new products coming out, new menu items, and special events. It is our way of asking for feedback and gathering good information from a trusted source, our established customer base. This is one of the simple ways we connect, where I can stay visible beyond just the general Facebook page and posts. We love the information we gather from this group of insiders.

Another powerful way I strive to remain visible is by working at least one full day a week inside the restaurant, and sometimes more depending on my schedule and responsibilities. For the first two years, I was in the building every day we were open. It was rare for me not to be onsite and working. But as our business has grown, the ranch has also grown, and I have been compelled to invest more time in keeping our ranch operation moving forward. If you come in to visit us for a meal on a Saturday or a holiday when we are open, you will most likely see me there taking orders, serving desserts, and stopping by tables for a chat. It is very important to me to continue to stay connected to our customers and the internal operation of the restaurant. I have found that people respond favorably to this visibility. No one really expects an owner to be around every open hour, but even the possibility of seeing the owner is encouraging for most people.

I also love to stay visible in the community. This is another thing that continues to be more difficult the busier life gets, but I love eating at our neighboring restaurants and then posting pictures of our meals there. Spending time in and around the community we serve is a great way to see people and build relationships. The owners who are around get to see us come in and support their business, and we love to encourage them with our presence and financial support. We always tip big! Not to come across as self-important, but we want to show our love for our friends (local restaurant owners whom we do not view as competition) and their work in our industry. Visibility is powerful because it shows you are present, and you are a member of the community.

Finally, I am visible online where I reply to our reviews and other comments and complaints. I believe it is of paramount importance to reply to each review and online comment made about my business. It is a challenging job that most either pawn off to a paid answering service or ignore altogether. Many of our good reviews are handled by my marketing team, but almost every bad review is answered by me. It really does not matter who replies to good reviews. But when it comes to specific complaints, I need to be the voice that people hear. If an apology is needed, it needs to come from me and no one else. Sometimes, wrong assumptions are made, and the reply needs to correct those misconceptions. Other times, mean-spirited words can be written, and a calm voice of ownership and understanding needs to be conveyed. I must admit that this is one of the hardest tasks I have. However, it is simply part of the job to be seen as the voice within these situations. This also brings about confidence to those coming behind and reading the discussion or negative review to know that the owner is concerned and available to make any response needed. It shows how much care and attention we invest in our business when customers see these situations being handled correctly.

In my opinion, a restaurant or other small business does themselves a disservice by ignoring online comments made about their business. It is your business, and reviews provide an opportunity to politely defend, respond to, or appreciate what others are saying about you and your life's work. Do not run from these opportunities to be visible. Use every check-in to say, "Thank you." Reply to every review. Say something nice to every kind word you are tagged in. It is a perfect way to show you care about your business and those who take the time to mention you.

All these efforts are part of a strong community connection. It is extremely important to be seen and heard as often as possible. In contrast, just think about the times you have seen these situations and no reply is ever made. No effort is seen to remedy or resolve those negative attacks on a business. It leaves you wondering if anyone really cares. We will never be free from some degree of negativity, no matter how hard we try, but no one will ever be able to say that we do not care about the customers and the experiences they have while dining with us!

As we were getting started (we had been open less than a month), a customer angrily posted about his experience on one of the most influential Facebook groups in our community. This guy posted a picture of his receipt. He wrote several paragraphs about how much we did not know and how bad his experience was. It blew up! Almost a thousand comments! I answered him very humbly and addressed a few of his concerns. Then I invited him back and asked him to give us another shot, "On the house. No charge." I am not sure if he ever came back. But the amount of business we had following that post and reply was overwhelming.

One of our most loyal customers told me recently that she visited us for the first time after that nasty post. I asked her what she remembered about it, and she said, "I could tell you cared about your business, and I had to come see what it was all about." Sherry has come in at least once a week, sometimes every other day, for the past five years. Everyone in the kitchen knows Sherry's order. They love her so much that they try to be the one who carries it out to her when it is ready to leave the kitchen.

Visibility is the key to sending the right message to those listening and paying attention. Regardless of the media used to communicate and regardless of the intent of the communication, the simple act of responding conveys the concern of the ownership.

Food is symbolic of love when words are inadequate.
~ Alan Wolfelt

From Crappy to Happy

THERE IS NOTHING more discouraging than a bad review. After working long hours, creating from the heart, just to have someone post negative comments for all to see is gut-wrenching. But what if it could be turned around into a groundbreaking idea?

When we first opened our restaurant, it was with a good plan but one without real-life experience. We asked folks to give us some time to learn, but it was hard to communicate something like that to the crowds of people who were coming in to eat with us. We had a good product; our ranch-fresh burgers were the best anyone had ever tasted (not bragging, just reporting what customers said, well, maybe bragging a little). Consistent execution was another story. We were learning as we went.

Our initial plan was to bag up the burgers and fries and then welcome people to sit and eat in our small dining area. Or they could walk a few steps down the trail behind us to the neighborhood park and grab a picnic table. Maybe they would like to catch a live concert a couple of blocks in the other direction just off the town square. We really thought that people would want to take their food to go. But, man, were we wrong!

We got gut-punched by the feedback. I recall one negative review that said, "Your burgers aren't that good and why do you stuff them in a sack even when you're eating inside the restaurant?" That was the one that changed our trajectory forever! This review was a crappy one for sure and a hard way to learn a lesson, but we learned the lesson well! We had never heard anyone complain about other burger shops that serve their burgers in a bag. But rather than being offended, we went to work on learning what we could from the feedback we received.

It was on that day that I decided to present our food differently. We began by locating the right bio-green paper plates with matching fry cups. Next, since our burgers would be displayed on a plate, they needed some branding! It was this intersection of bad and good where greatness was born. We designed and ordered the first "WELLS" bun brander. Little did I know just how big of an impact these changes would have on our overall marketing and success.

Now when our burgers left the kitchen, they looked amazing on the plate. It was also eye-catching to see our name literally branded on top of the bun. While this branding idea had been done by other burger restaurants, for some reason, it was a giant success for us! Now before people took their first bite, they pulled out their phone for a quick picture and, many times, a social media tag! Our most helpful organic marketing move was born from an almost tearfully negative experience. One simple change created a historic win that keeps helping us advance every day.

Anyone who is alive right now knows that reviews are part of this generation. Smartphones make it easy to leave feedback with a simple touch of the screen. I believe that people who are unhappy may be quicker to leave a review than a satisfied customer. When people are unhappy, they seem to want to strike back, while happy customers may come back for years without ever leaving any reviews at all. Some quick research says that 95% of people with a bad experience are likely to share a bad review, while only 87% will share a good experience.

My philosophy on bad reviews is that they are most likely submitted by three general types of customers: 1) the unhappy person, 2) the disgruntled person, and 3) the disappointed person. All three *can* and often *will* lash out to bite you.

The *unhappy person* is simply unhappy with life. He or she walks in with a frown on their face and a negative posture. Unfortunately, there is not much we can do to fix these customers. Life is just not good to them, and they are looking to spread some unhappiness with their review of you. Sometimes it is as simple as their spouse forcing them to be there against their will, and there will be no winner in that situation. They would simply rather be anywhere else. All you can do is hope they cannot turn on a computer or that they are unable to find the review sites.

I watch for these folks and try to help them smile or lighten up, but usually, their state of mind runs deeper than a guy behind a counter with a smile or a waiter with a good joke. They are truly unhappy people being forced into your life.

The *disgruntled person* has had an unfortunate experience with the visit and is irritated and not afraid to show it. These are many times some of those *unhappy people* too, but you have at least done something to cause their disgruntled behavior. Sometimes a free item or reimbursed check can help save a bad review if the restaurant finds a satisfactory method of resolution. But even then, it may not ever be a five-star review. Sometimes the most innocent mistakes can cause a horrible reaction or overreaction. It happens to the very best establishments, and sometimes these negative happenings are completely unavoidable, like running out of an item or an accidental kitchen mistake such as failing to include bacon or cheese on a burger. All we can do is recognize the situation and try to make it right.

Finally, there is the *disappointed person*. He or she may have had their expectations too high or had the wrong idea about you before coming inside. Unrealistic expectations are a hard thing for people to get beyond in their mind. When an establishment has been hyped up by friends, great reviews, or even the media, there can be an unfortunate letdown for some. When I recognize this over-excited behavior in a customer, I will say something like, "You know it's just a burger," or "You know our food doesn't perform miracles." Something jovial may bring their expectations back into reality to avoid an unnecessary letdown. These disappointments also happen when kitchens have off-days and fail to perform at their best every moment of every day.

Disappointments can arise when customers' expectations are not in tune with reality, such as the expectation that servers will simply know the customers' unspoken wishes. Many times, these assumptions are made by the customer and can turn into disappointments. The harsh reality is that the business cannot do a thing about this type of disappointment. We know that no one wins every day. No sports team wins every game.

Life has its letdowns and disappointments. It is going to happen, and people will leave negative feedback at times when they are disappointed, regardless of whose fault it might be. All we can do is address the issues we learn about and try not to be discouraged if there is little we can do to avoid the problem.

When replying to negative reviews, my practice is to speak kindly, but I always try to consider the future review readers more so than the person who wrote the review. Chances are you will not remedy a bad experience with a review reply of any kind. The damage has already been done, and moving on is the best policy. But to that next review reader, there is an opportunity to redeem yourself in some way. You can be gracious. You can reply with humility. You can impress the next reader and perhaps even gain a future customer with your level-headed response.

And then there are times when reviews are so ridiculous they are joke-worthy. There have been a few times that we even turned the bad review into a t-shirt. We sell a one-star Google review shirt that states the text of the review on the front, "Overpriced Burger, Absolutely No Flavor," along with the Google page's one-star graphic layout. But on the back, it states our comeback, "Voted Best Burger Every Year!" Some reviews are so silly you just must laugh!

Reviews are important and powerful; we take them very seriously. Just for reference, we have maintained a 4.6-star average on Google and a 4.5-star average on Yelp with almost two thousand reviews given. To put this into perspective, the national average for independent restaurants on Google's rating platform is a 4.2-star average, and restaurant chains come in at a low 3.8-star average. For Yelp, all I was able to find is a small blurb about the national average being between a 3 and 4-star review. Yelp is not as open with their averages as Google seems to be. So, by the national standard, we are doing very well!

An interesting tidbit about reviews and their importance is that it takes 40 positive reviews to undo the damage of one negative review.

Everyone absolutely hates to see the negative comments and low ratings come in, but it helps to look at them through this new lens we have discussed. Maybe there is something to be learned and maybe not. Perhaps that person's life is in such shambles that they view every experience as woefully negative. Be glad your life is not like theirs. Never sink to your most negative comment, and never fully believe your best and most positive compliment. Somewhere in between is closest to your reality. Enjoy the opportunity to start over again tomorrow.

While we all strive for straight five-star reviews, there is something believable about the mix of both positive and negative reviews that are seen when looking at a business. If all the reviews are perfect, it begs the question of true reality. Were those reviews all submitted by family members? Were they paid reviewers? So having some negativity sprinkled in paints a realistic picture.

There will always be negative people in the world ready to take their frustrations out on someone else (and today, that someone else could be us), but we continue to "Strive for Five" every single day we open our doors. Most reviews can be helpful if viewed in the correct context and approached with humility. We have seen some of our most grave mistakes called out in hurtful reviews, but if we can make a change and be better, then we have been helped by something that was intended to hurt. It is all perspective. It is all about a desire to be the best we can be for our customers every day.

If you really want to make the biggest impact possible to help a small business, find reasons to praise them for what they do well. Leave a five-star review and explain why you feel it is deserved. But there is another level of reviews out there that many do not think about. I simply call it the "Updated Review." Regardless of the number of stars you originally gave the business, you can always go back and update your review! These are the most powerful reviews on the internet. When someone comes back to a review a year later and says, "This place has become our favorite restaurant in town!" or perhaps they say something like, "Still amazing, still turning out the best products every time we are there!" These show progress and indicate a successful history! They are worth their weight in gold.

One of my favorite updated reviews started out as a negative review, maybe a two-star, which said ours was not his favorite burger and that we over-cooked our meat. So, I reached out to him privately and offered to buy him another burger the way he wanted it cooked. He returned and loved his burger that we prepared cooked medium. After a few more visits, he updated his original review with a kind five-star full of praise for our food and customer service. This review showed much more about us than just a good or bad product. It shows the world what a great business we strive to operate! Anytime you are impressed with a place of business, again and again, consider leaving them the most awesome review possible – the updated review.

> *People got opinions, that's all they've got.*
> ~ *Augustus (Gus) McCrae*

Complainers Welcome

WHEN I WAS a young man, our family often drove past a certain steakhouse just outside of downtown Dallas. Every time we passed it, my dad would say something about trying it out someday. One night, I decided to take my girlfriend out to this steakhouse. I told Dad about it, and he was excited for us! She and I had a nice time, but the food was not as good as we expected, and being young and on a date, we simply finished our meal, paid the bill and tip, and left.

When I got home later that night, Dad asked how we enjoyed our dinner. I told him it was quite disappointing and that I would not be going back. He immediately asked a very important question that I will never forget. He asked if I had told a manager how I felt. I laughed and said something like, "No, the manager did not even know we were there." He looked very intently at me and said, "You owe them that feedback." Wow! What? I spent my own money, and the food was "crap."

He said something that I still remember every time I sit down in a restaurant. He said, "If you are not honest with them, they will never be successful." Then he told me something crazy! He said, "You have to go back." Why would I ever do that? He explained that I could not simply abandon a place of business without giving them an opportunity to remedy the problem. He continued, "Go back. And if it's bad, let them fix it. The best thing you can do for them is give them a second chance and honest feedback."

That talk has stayed with me for decades, and he was right. How could I refuse to give a business a second chance and then take a verbal hatchet to them anytime they come up in conversation? How dare I write a bad thing about them online if I have not tried to help them be better in person?

Has this happened to you? You anticipate the experience of trying a new restaurant. You have told others that you are going. You may have already checked in on social media, and people are expecting a report.

The food arrives, and the fries are cold, or the meat is overcooked. Perhaps you used the restroom, and the hand towel dispenser was empty. Then the question arises, do you complain or just smile and work through your problems quietly? Do you just make a generic reply on social media, or do you ignore that you ever checked in on Facebook in the first place?

As a business owner, I will stand up and make it clear for all to hear. Please, please, please, complain! Anyone who cares about his business, his customers, and those who will become customers cares about *every little thing* within his control. I promise you that after a business owner has mortgaged, saved, risked, and sacrificed, he cares about you! Your satisfaction is ultimately tied to his being able to continue his dream. It is never wrong to respectfully speak up about a real problem you have encountered. It is actually both welcomed and appreciated.

Recently, I walked by a table to check on a couple eating with us, and the man had finished his food. He had his paper tray and napkins neatly stacked in front of him on the table. As I talked with him about his Keto bun and its carbohydrate count, I noticed that the lady with him was pinching small bites off her burger. She had not eaten even half of it. I asked her if there was something wrong with her burger. She made a face and then said, "Do you have a house seasoning on the meat?" I answered that we did, and she told me it was too strong for her tastebuds. She then explained that since her battle with cancer and radiation treatments, her taste had been greatly affected. I reached out and took her by the hand and said, "Ma'am, there is no reason in the world why you should have to eat anything you do not like. All you have to do is request no seasoning." I asked for her burger and then proceeded to have a fresh burger made to her liking.

A few minutes later, I was talking with another group of customers by the front door as the couple with the remade burger was leaving. The lady interrupted me, and this time, she grabbed my hand and said with a big smile, "That was the best burger I have ever had! Thank you for making me a new one I could enjoy." I reminded her simply to request anything she wanted done to her burger the next time she came in, and she assured me that there would be a next time.

What could have been a bad review or a lost customer turned into a success story because we were able to correct the issue while the customer was present. I believe it is true for all small business owners that we would much rather hear of an issue in person than hear of that issue in a bad review. So, please complain!

Just last week, we received a two-star review, and the reviewer did not even complain about our food or service. It was a review of our restroom. This guy even posted pictures of the restroom. So, I asked our managers, who were on duty that day, and they had never received a complaint about the restroom. This guy did not bother to speak to anyone who could have remedied his complaint, but rather, he posted his complaint publicly to live forever on the internet.

For those who have never been inside our old house-converted restaurant, we have one family restroom, so it gets a great deal of use. We also found, when we investigated his pictures and complaint, that what he saw was water damage from a recent leak in our air conditioning system rather than a "restroom issue."

The restroom is repainted and neatly caulked now, but a simple question would have been welcomed by any staff member or manager who would have happily explained the water damage. And they would still have sent someone to double-check the tidiness of the facilities.

When customers exert no personal effort that would enable the small business to remedy a bad situation, it is cowardly. Please have the gumption to speak up inside the business when your input can be constructive to help the business grow. I do not understand the concept that says keeping quiet is polite or good manners. When a person purchases a product or service, he has every right to be heard by management and to expect top-notch treatment. I am convinced that we would have better businesses if our customers would communicate better with us.

Please understand that I am not saying that there is never a place for negative reviews. There is definitely an appropriate time and place for a negative experience to be made public. But in my opinion and practice, that review is only warranted after giving a business multiple visits and only after trying to communicate your concerns with management.

There was a local chain restaurant where my brother and I enjoyed eating breakfast, and we frequented this place for years. Something happened to their management and then the crew, and over the span of a year, the restaurant became deplorable. Things finally reached a point where I pulled out my phone and gave them a one-star review with a stern warning to others to stay away. This review was written after months of watching for improvement, speaking to management, and even calling their corporate office. However, changes were not made, and to this day, they struggle to stay open in spite of their busy highway location.

A bad review warning should never be given after only one or two visits. Every business struggles at times. We should remember the people who own the business, their children, and the employees who depend on that business for their livelihood. Even if you decide that a business is not for you, there is no need to automatically leave a negative review. Have mercy where you can. No business is perfect, and life can be tough for all of us. Try to make a business better first!

Kindness begins with the understanding that we all struggle.
~ Charles Glassman

Trust and Loyalty

I WAS IN the restaurant every day we were open for the first two years. It was crucial that I be there to build a culture of our internal processes along with our external customer service expectations. It was the best decision I could have made. Have you been to restaurants and other types of businesses and wondered if anyone in the building knew what was supposed to be happening? It was of paramount importance to me to help establish the type of business I wanted to see and this also built great leaders within the staff as well.

By being present, I was able to teach others on the management team what the Wells expectations are on every subject, every recipe, and a variety of situations. Now I am able to spend more time working the ranch side of the business, knowing that the time I invested up front established leaders and processes that can be trusted today. While I receive an occasional phone call or text, the majority of the operation runs smoothly. Trust empowers great leaders. I know they know exactly what to do in almost any situation, and this knowledge allows me time to be useful in other areas that require my skillset.

Many companies fail because the owners cannot trust the management to operate the business without them being present. Trust is a two-way street. It takes confidence in both directions for it to work. The working relationship must be mature enough to handle the expectations that will arise. I am grateful for a team of people who enjoy conducting business in the Wells culture that we have established. We agree that this is the best way to operate, and it is a beautiful thing to come together and serve.

Not only does management require trust, but the customer must participate in this process of trust as well. We have some of the greatest customers in the world! We hate making mistakes, but we appreciate the feedback from our trusted customers when things go wrong. Periodically, I will receive a private message or phone call that says, "Mr. Wells, we ordered to-go, and when we got home, we noticed something was wrong with our order. We just wanted you to know so that your kitchen is aware." Now, if they did not trust our motives to serve, this mistake could have been posted publicly as a bad review or a nasty comment on social media. But with our customers, their loyalty improves our process going forward.

Thinking back about our customers and their relationship with us, once or twice we received a message that our front door was standing open when we were supposed to be closed! It turned out to be a grocery delivery both times, so everything was okay. But the loyalty and concern our customers have for us is still amazing!

During the Covid shutdowns, we were told almost daily by our loyal customers that we were not going to falter and close our doors. They were going to keep us open. I was told by several people that they had written a schedule for each evening meal. They intended to order from their favorite restaurants until restaurants could reopen. I had one regular customer call me aside one afternoon and ask if we were making it okay financially and if we needed anything. I said we were doing well and making it. He then told me that if we needed an interest-free bridge loan at any point to please contact him. He was not going to allow us to be hurt by the situation. That is customer trust! That is customer loyalty! This is what matters when you really look at the core of a business. To hold such vast customer trust and loyalty is one of the highest honors we could ever experience.

I have made the mistake of working with people
solely based upon their brain, but I have found it is
more important that they have a good heart.
~ Elon Musk

CHAPTER FOUR
WELLS WINNING CULTURE

First and Lasting Impressions

I AM ALWAYS EXCITED to try a new eatery! Before I arrive at a new place, I usually check out some reviews and look over some food pictures to see what the restaurant offers as their specialty. Many times, I have a top menu item in mind before ever seeing their physical menu. I can be prepared for the prices, atmosphere, serving style, and ethnicity of their offerings. I can also know if alcohol is served or if it is a BYOB-style restaurant. There is much that can be learned prior to a first visit.

As I approach a business for the first time, I always take into consideration the front door. Is it clean? Is it functioning correctly? Most importantly, what does it communicate to me?

The front door can say so much before you ever walk inside. Is it welcoming, or is it shunning? I do not mind seeing the standard credit card sticker or even a neighborhood favorite sticker or a Yelp sticker. However, I dislike the negative stickers and what I call "do not enter" signs. *No outside food.* Ok, that is almost a given these days. Or *No Checks!* How about, *No shoes, no shirt, no service?* I would think that is standard as well, except maybe if you are on a beach. However, the message I hate to see the most is: *We reserve the right to refuse service to anyone.* What? You are going to lead with that? I have been in the restaurant business for several years now, and never once has any one of these pre-warned problems ever actually been an issue. No customer has ever placed an order and then pulled out their checkbook to start writing a check. In fact, no one has ever asked if we take checks. So, what is the point of such signage on the front door? In my opinion, I believe that our message must stay positive and inviting.

I wish owners would consider the customer's first impression and re- think all the chest-beating warning signs. When was the last time you walked up to a fine steakhouse door and saw anything just mentioned? The classier the establishment, the more attention curb appeal receives. If a problem arises, we will deal with that specific person and situation at that time. I refuse to present that as an ultimatum to everyone who walks through my door. I want people to feel welcome the entire time they are with us, from their entry through the front door until they leave through that same door.

Another "first" that happens after getting past the front door involves the very first person we meet. Often, we encounter the least qualified, least mature person on the staff, the host or hostess. That person is usually the least trained, the most sensitive to stress, and most likely to abuse his or her newly acquired authority. If we are not careful, we will entrust our most valuable commodity, hungry customers, to someone who seems to care the least. Many times the host or hostess is the least invested staff person in the entire company.

I have seen the host or hostess greet guests who plan to spend hundreds of dollars by telling them that the wait for a table is three or four times the actual wait time. Simply because the lobby is full, they do not care to search for available seating. Many times, potential customers are given inaccurate information because people are not properly trained, or even worse, they do not want more guests piling into the already busy restaurant. It is a standard obstacle to overcome that would be simple to remedy. Generally, the classier the restaurant, the better trained and more mature the host staff is. In fact, in recent memory, some of our best dining experiences have been in restaurants with older hosts who take pride in their employer and the establishment they represent.

One of the fine dining restaurants we frequent has the best hostess I have ever seen. She is probably in her late sixties and is always pleasant. She will stand and talk about the owner and the way the restaurant works as if she is part of the ownership, but actually, she is just very good at her job. She keeps everyone informed about their remaining wait time and will even let you know how many tables she needs to seat before you. It is an amazing thing to watch such grace and poise as she protects the reputation and projects the attitude of the establishment. I cannot imagine an inexperienced person doing anything like she does. She is a true asset to the ownership of a great restaurant.

The other "first" impressions come from the waitstaff and management. Any first contact with the customers must be positive and informative. Genuine conversation and connection are imperative to a meaningful exchange. Eye contact and real interaction will set people up for a positive experience. People are choosing to come to your table to enjoy a meal with other significant people in their lives. We must be our best every day.

Many mid-level steakhouses seem to be meeting a quota each night with generic table visits that happen extremely informally and sometimes without breaking stride. They bump the table with their fist gently and ask if everything is okay. No sincerity, no eye contact, just checking the table off their list. It is better for a manager not to come by at all if he or she is not genuine. A sincere concern cannot be delivered on the run. It seems to be nothing more than an assigned job that must happen at every table and for every visit. This practice can be counterproductive, in my opinion, especially if it is done with insincerity.

At my restaurant, I make a point to stop and visit every table possible. Sometimes we talk longer when we get into a genuine conversation. Sometimes it is simply a quick "hello." If the customers are doing well and enjoying their food, there is no need to stand and awkwardly try to force a conversation. But when I am at a table, my conversations are authentic. I feel comfortable chatting with the customers, and my message to everyone is some form of gratitude, such as "Thank you for coming" or "Thank you for choosing us today." And then I make sure they are being well taken care of. "Can I get you anything? Would you care for some house-made pie or cobbler today?" Table touches are needed, but they only seem to work when the person doing them genuinely cares. People can tell the heart and motivation of the conversation. Show them the concern they deserve, and true friendship and loyalty will be born.

> *A good first impression can work wonders.*
> *~ J.K. Rowling*

Excellence

JUST BECAUSE I own a restaurant does not mean it belongs to me. That may be a shocking statement, but it is absolutely true. My restaurant belongs to every customer who chooses to spend their hard-earned money with us to purchase our food and feed their families. I am humbled by the success we have seen in the time we have been serving our community. We have won almost every award given for burgers in our area since we opened only five years ago. We do not take a single accolade lightly.

While we have never pursued any culinary industry awards, we have been showered with "Local Best Awards" from day one. The powerful thing about these awards is their source. These are public-opinion awards, peoples' choice awards, and readers' choice awards, and they are extremely important to us because of the people who choose us, our customers. And that commitment is mutual. We are just as committed to each of them with the excellence we pursue every day.

The sign over the door may say my name, but the moment people stop walking through that door, it is all just an evaporating dream. So, everything we do has the customer at heart and in mind, and those wonderful people deserve our very best. Excellence at every turn is the baseline effort that our customers deserve. We find the very best ingredients, partners, and employees we can because our customer family is worth the effort. Many restaurant owners may buy the cheapest products possible to save every dollar they can, even at the expense of quality and flavor. We have always bought the best products we can get. For example, some may say, "It's just mayonnaise." But when you are a hamburger restaurant, mayonnaise is served on most burgers. It is a small thing that is everywhere you look on our menu. It matters.

As I mentioned in a previous chapter, we include every cut on the side of beef in our hamburger meat. The question could be asked, "Who would know if I kept back a rib-eye every so often?" Maybe no one else would ever know, but I would. My kids would. When we say we include every

64

prime cut, that is exactly what we do. There is a saying that we try to live up to every day: "Character is what we do when no one is looking." Most of the key decisions of excellence are made behind kitchen doors. The customer is never directly aware of these decisions, but they have to live with them every time they sit at our table.

One of my personal pet peeves is when I walk up to a fountain drink machine to find the mix of syrup and soda is out of calibration. This is an inexcusable lack of excellence that costs nothing to remedy. With a simple phone request, the drink distributor will schedule a free calibration visit. It only takes a matter of minutes to have a drink machine operating perfectly according to factory specifications. The reason the trip and service are free is simple. The drink supplier desires for their drink flavors to taste correct. It hurts both the restaurant and the drink company for a drink to taste bad. This is a simple example of striving for excellence, and it only has to happen about once a year in most cases for every drink in the fountain to taste perfect.

While we are discussing drinks and easy fixes, another issue I see is the lack of sweeteners available. It is not 1982 anymore. We can have more than white sugar and Sweet'N Low for our customers. It does not cost a restaurant anymore to offer Splenda, Equal, or Truvia. But it is such a nice gesture when the customers see their preferred sweetener is available to them. Excellence is going beyond what is required and showing those who choose you that they matter. We do our best every day to provide every little thing we can along with all the big things we already do for them. This includes small things such as the quality of hand towels in the restroom and even the ply of our toilet paper!

Speaking of hand towels, does anyone find it inconvenient to wash your hands and then look over to see a hand air dryer on the wall of a restroom? What about the water on the countertop, the wet floor, and the dripping doorknob? Does it seem like the establishment is trying to be frugal at the customer's expense? At one time hand dryers may have been considered more sanitary, but that has since been called into question. (They have been proven to retain and circulate airborne bathroom bacteria.) Maybe it is just my dislike for hand dryers that causes me to feel that way. But good quality products in every area of business always convey an attitude of excellence.

One of the areas of excellence that may be the hardest to maintain is executional consistency or, in other words, the stamina to press for excellence every day. Anyone can do something right once, or for one day, or maybe even for one year. However, we must press tirelessly forward every day to be truly excellent in every way and be consistent with an aptitude for excellence in every regard. The entire team and every station must be onboard, and this unity only comes from a culture of excellence.

We strive to be our very best, knowing that it is literally impossible to be perfect. The great Vince Lombardi phrased this pursuit well: "Perfection is not attainable, but if we chase perfection, we can catch excellence."

Excellence in all things matters. That should be our promise to our customers!

To be successful is to be helpful, caring, and constructive, to make everything and everyone you touch a little bit better.
~ Norman Vincent Peale

Foundational Marketing

I HAVE MENTIONED a variety of marketing techniques already; however, you may not have noticed them because they were not labeled *marketing techniques*. They were simply part of what we do every day. So many people think of marketing as a certain set of actions such as renting a billboard, running a radio ad, setting up a Facebook page, or spending funds on ad campaigns. All these tasks are marketing activities, and we do them on a regular basis. However, I believe marketing is so much more than a list of static actions. The foundation must be established before any real business success can be built.

True marketing is any opportunity to get our brand out in front of a customer. So, in essence, I view every customer relationship as part of our foundational marketing strategy. Why? Because every time we serve a happy customer and they walk out the door satisfied, he or she is a potential talking advertisement. Someone may ask that customer where they ate lunch, what their favorite restaurant is, or where they could find a good hamburger, and if their answer is "Wells," then that one interaction is more powerful than ten billboards or a thousand radio commercials. Really everything we do each day inside the business is foundational marketing, and that is what makes our outside marketing work. When new customers walk in and experience the culture of excellence and value we have established, all the marketing efforts come together successfully.

The best marketing strategies are probably pointless unless the experience inside the business is as great as the hype outside the business. Businesses can really do themselves a disservice when they spend time and money on outside marketing efforts while the inside processes are not proven or not working well. Marketing a business that is providing a bad service or product is counterproductive in every way. Even if you do persuade a customer to come in and make a purchase, it will most likely be a negative experience. Then that customer becomes a "negative talking experience" to those they encounter. It is imperative that the business operates correctly first before any marketing can prove to be successful.

Over the past several years the Dallas area has become home to several power-chain restaurants from the northeastern states. When they start construction, it always causes a whirlwind of excitement. The news outlets talk them up, and of course, the transplants from those states are talking about them nonstop. There is the inevitable countdown of days until the first location opens, and then the diehards camp out overnight to be the first in the door. The marketing is fierce, and the excitement is real, but then the performance inside must hold up or the entire build-up is for naught. The inside processes are usually not robust enough to handle the level of hype and marketing that has been amassing outside the kitchen.

Recently, my family had been waiting for one of these transplant chains to calm down enough to get inside within an hour. We finally visited on a Tuesday afternoon around 5 o'clock. We stood in line for serval minutes, and then we ordered and waited for a while for the order to be called. Once our number was called, we walked up to retrieve the order. But the order was incomplete. We had to argue with the staff, with our receipt in hand. We had incorrect items, items completely missing, and one item not even on the order! Then we were told that we must go back through the long line to reorder the missing item. To make our experience even less fun, we never got the correct desserts.

Now I understand that this was a new location, and I would never leave a bad review. I am not mentioning them by name here because I understand what happened. They did not have their foundation set. They were still establishing employees and training on the proper processes that have made them successful up North. But how many customers are they running off during these first several months of being open because they are not established yet? It seems that their outside marketing is overpowering their foundational ability to please a customer base inside.

With all of that said, we spend money on marketing to expose our community to our business. Outside marketing is a necessary part of any good business plan. Regardless of how many people you expect to know that you are open, there seem to be thousands more people who have never stopped in once. So, you must continue to reach for them.

For those existing customers, your marketing serves as a reminder for them to return. It takes a constant effort to remind current customers and expose new people to continue to fill your business seats. We have customers almost every day who say, "I never knew this place was here until I saw an ad on Facebook," or "I heard about you from a friend."

One day I was working in the restaurant, and a customer came in wearing one of our hats. I mentioned that I liked his hat. Then he smiled and told me about his trip to The State Fair of Texas. While in the massive crowd, he spotted two different "Wells" hats! When you think about our restaurant being located about twenty-five miles outside of downtown Dallas, and we are in the far northeast corner of the Metroplex, you can only describe the spotting of two hats as amazing! His seeing our hats out there is exciting and communicated to me the reach of our word of mouth. That is powerful marketing. When customers choose to wear our merchandise, it speaks loudly to their loyalty and their testimony of what we provide, and it sets a foundation the rest of our marketing can be built upon.

Once the right foundation is established in-house, the outside efforts will be much more fruitful. Many will remember the massive Chick-fil-A campaign with the spotted cows saying "Eat Mor Chikin" that came out in the mid-90s. It has been called the most successful ad campaign of our generation, but it would have never worked if the culture of Chick-fil-A was not already perfected and ready to back up the efforts of the outside marketing campaign. It took a solid foundation of word-of-mouth and consistent execution inside each store before the outside marketing could work.

In summary, if the foundation of the business is not solid, no amount of marketing will make a business work long term, and by the same truth, if the foundation is strong, every effort to add to the business will potentially build up and provide added success.

> *Marketing is everything ... everything is marketing.*
> ~ Regis McKenna

Community Partnership

I KNOW WE may have heard it said, and perhaps we have even said it ourselves: "The restaurant industry is a highly competitive business!" However, I submit to you that competition is a phantom ghost that does not exist in my mind. Competition gets wrongfully blamed for failures that could easily be remedied if clearly seen and addressed.

Perhaps some businesses view others as competition. But I choose to view life and business differently. What if my "competitors" were simply my neighbors offering a different take on a dish, cuisine, or service that I also provide? What if they were simply a friend offering another option to choose from when the family is deciding where they will go eat tonight?

It is not personal in my house when it is time to decide where to eat out for family dinner. It usually goes like this, "You want pizza, tacos, wings, or fajitas?" And then the discussion ping pongs for five minutes until everyone is frustrated and hungrier than when we started talking about where to eat. It has never been said in my house, "Well, we can't eat at that place because that guy is our competition, and we dislike his family!" Not a single time has anything like that been spoken in our home during a decision to visit a place of business of any kind. So why would restaurateurs and business owners feel that way when thinking of their neighboring owners? It is silly to think like this! And it can be damaging to a community if people act like this. There is no such thing as competition, only options and opinions for what someone is hungry for today.

If a business finds itself overlooked, or not busy, it is not the customers' fault for not choosing them. It is not the fault of the neighbor down the street who is receiving the business. In all honesty, the problem can only be addressed in-house. Why are people passing your establishment and paying someone else for that same service? Is it a lack of marketing, poor customer service, high prices, or bad quality? There must be a reason, but it is probably not the fault of competition. That is a simple but incorrect excuse.

70

For years I have made it a practice to frequent as many local restaurants as possible. I always take time to speak with the staff and the owner, if he or she is around. I always try my best to catch a second of the management's time to say, "Hello." Once the food arrives at the table, I take out my phone and try to get the very best picture I can of their food and post it on my personal social media accounts.

I love supporting my friends and neighbors in the hospitality business. The moment we introduce ourselves and put a name and face with the *competition*, they are no longer our competition but our friends we are cheering for and wanting to see succeed. As business owners, it is our responsibility to build up our community. I believe true change in any community comes from real relationships, open communication, and genuine gratitude toward each other. We all bring something unique to the marketplace, and that is the real beauty of our community! We have enough unfair treatment and negativity in life without creating it with people who are working as hard as we do each day. I love seeing my neighbors as friends rather than *my competition*.

I will never forget meeting Stu. He was a local guy who had a tea shop several blocks from our restaurant. He would come in and rave about our quality. The burger was the best. The fries were the best. But he would not drink our tea. He would say, "You must do better on your tea. It's the one thing you are not doing with excellence." I made excuses about not having enough counter space and that we had a good system of flavored, pre-mixed bagged tea. Now that I think back on it, I am embarrassed about what we were serving. However, I was new to the business and thought we were covered on beverages from my other suppliers. Finally, Stu invited me to his shop one day. He called about three o'clock one afternoon and said to come over because he had paired a couple of teas for me to sample. He just wanted me to taste the difference. I jumped in my truck and hurried over to his place to try these "better teas." And I must admit that he was not just kind of right; he was absolutely right! I stepped up to his counter, and he poured me a glass of ice-cold peach mango tea. Wow! So crisp and delicious. It did not even need sweeteners. It was a true blend of fresh tea leaves and flowers to make the perfect flavored brewed tea.

I loved it, but I still did not have counter space for a brewing station and tea urns. Or at least I did not think I had the space. The next day Stu walked into my place with a tape measure and said, "If I can find a unit that will fit in this space, will you buy it?" I agreed, and he told me that he would set it up and calibrate it. What a deal!

As you can guess, within a few weeks we had a double tea urn and brewing station, along with the best tea in the city. We have now won awards for "best tea" and have beat out several tea shops and even boba houses with our specially blended peach mango tea from Stu, his amazing wife, and their crew from across town.

When I compare the price of the bagged tea product we started with and what we spend today on our teas, I know I could save money by using a lower quality product, but our customers and our standard of excellence simply would not allow that ever to happen. We are doing so well because we serve great products, and our customers are worth it! I am forever grateful for Stu's persistence and love for our place. He and his family are still dear friends and tremendous supporters of our restaurant.

We also partner with several other local companies who share the same high standards of excellence. For instance, our ice cream is supplied by a local creamery just down the road. Their ice cream is an amazing addition to our house-made desserts and the reason our shakes are the best you can find anywhere!

One of my favorite collaborations is when we partner with other local restaurants to bring our beef onto their menu in a creative way. We have partnered with a local upscale pizza restaurant and provided our whole-ground beef for their monthly specials. Later we were astonished to hear that our hamburger beef pizza was one of their best-selling specials of the year.

Every once in a while, we will create a burger just for fun. For a while, we had a burger that featured the barbeque brisket from a local smokehouse and our house-made barbeque sauce with their pickled onions. It was amazing and worked to better both of our businesses. Working together provided a unique opportunity for businesses to talk proudly about another business. There have been several partnerships such as the local donut shop for a donut burger and the local bagel shop for a bagel burger. Everyone wins! Anytime we can support other local businesses it is always a win-win situation.

Instead of competing for business, we should work together to build each other's businesses.

It really comes down to the principle that says, "We all do better working together than we do standing alone." I am convinced that the better we do collectively, in our downtown, the better we will do individually. When we build up our local area restaurants, we foster more traffic, more excitement, and more customers for everyone. A family may drive downtown to visit a neighboring restaurant today. They may see my restaurant and decide to return tomorrow. Or I may attract a new customer today as they make their way downtown, and they may see another new restaurant that they have never visited. There is a synergy in success. The better our whole area performs, the more success we will all see. Abundance is better than scarcity. There are enough people looking for quality food and hospitality to go around.

In my opinion, there is no such thing as competition.

> *A candle loses nothing by lighting another candle.*
> *~ James Keller*

Menu Harmony

HAVE YOU EVER looked at a menu and tried to make sense of the pricing? I do not know about you, but I get frustrated when I see a side of white rice for four dollars when I know that it costs next to nothing. I was in a restaurant the other day, and their menu made no sense whatsoever. Prices were not even close to a pattern. The only explanation I can imagine is that people just make up the prices arbitrarily.

Recently I noticed the burger price at a local diner. Their burger was listed at $6.50, but the double was $12.98 Why? Maybe some people do not look at the prices when they order. One could almost order two burgers for the price of one with a double patty.

Another inconsistency is where meals cost a certain amount, but to order it à la carte would cost literally two or three times what the meal alone costs. I really do not understand why restaurants do this. Why not figure the food cost correctly and make the menu prices congruent across the board?

Currently, at a major fast food restaurant, you can order a side of a single patty sausage for $2.19. However, you can order two sausage biscuits for $2.40. That is a total of two biscuits and two sausage patties for almost the same price as the one side of sausage. This makes no sense, especially for an international chain restaurant.

I do not eat eggs for breakfast, strange I know, but I just do not. So many times, I will request to substitute hash browns for eggs. However, many places will not make this substitution without an upcharge. Why not? A few pieces of potato are always cheaper than two eggs. Why not make the customer happy and make a few more cents on the order with a downward substitution? They are saving two eggs for someone who actually wants them.

At my restaurant we have all items priced. For instance, an egg currently costs a dollar fifty, and so do two strips of crispy bacon. It does not matter what you get them on or what you add them to. The price of our food does not magically change because it is located on a different page of the menu.

If someone wants to substitute an item like a bun style, that is an easy request for us. Some people ask for a lettuce wrap rather than a bread bun, so we are happy to give someone two pieces of lettuce and not charge more. We are keeping a more expensive bun back for the next order. Of course, we do have an upcharge for specialty buns that we order from local bakeries, such as gluten-free and low-carb buns.

It is also heart-wrenching to see prices go up and portions go down. I believe this is one of the single most frustrating things restaurants do. Eventually, it catches up with them and causes them to lose business or even shut down. Customers must see a value on their plate. We recently had to increase our prices. I hated to do it; but as they say in politics, "It's the economy, stupid." Our patty weight was one-third pound which translates to 5.3 ounces. When we increased our price, even though it was justified by the rising cost of goods, we also increased our patty size to 5.5 ounces simply because I refused to go up on price and not do my best to give more value on the plate. While we are on this subject, let me add that owners cannot keep buying cheaper ingredients without the customer noticing they are getting cheap and offering less on the plate. My kitchen is not allowed to downgrade our grocery items for any reason.

We utilize multiple suppliers in case one is out of our items. We can buy from another vendor that week and keep our kitchen quality where it needs to be. The customer is smart and probably will not tell you that the bacon has gotten paper thin or that the mayonnaise tastes cheap. However, it does not mean they are not disappointed with the changes. They may simply not return.

The menu must make sense. Pricing and value must be there for the customer to return and tell others about your restaurant. If we can keep a fair value on the plate with a quality product to enjoy, business will remain strong and growing. People support passion, and nothing shows our passion like the quality we serve and the consistency we offer each day. But it must make sense.

Simplicity is the ultimate sophistication.
~ Leonardo DaVinci

Discount Games

PERHAPS YOU HAVE seen: Buy one meal, get one free Monday, or 30% off every meal Tuesday. Or how about half-priced appetizers after 9 o'clock p.m.?

These gimmicks are meant to entice an extra visit and get you in the door when you need some help with balancing the family budget. But to me, they always seem cheap and telling of the real food cost associated with those advertised items. Discounts have a way of diminishing the value of a product.

My brain always says, "If you can sell that steak dinner for that discounted price today, you are either going broke today or making a killing every other day." This kind of inside exposure is not necessary to share with the world. Everyone knows that menu prices are marked up from bare costs to cover overhead and to make some level of profit. However, no one wants to be reminded of the real food cost. Take the American pizza, for example. We really do not want to think of the food cost of pizza when buying one. I recently looked it up on Google and found the hard cost of a medium pizza is still less than a dollar, yet the national average price for a medium pizza is just under $20 these days. (I think I may be in the wrong business!)

It is my opinion that we should price our menu fairly and stay out of the discount game. Most businesses doing well do not need to discount their items like a used car lot trying to draw in one more customer before they close forever. If we stop and think about it, when is the last time a highly successful business model like Raising Cane's offered a special discounted price on The Caniac Combo? Or when has In-N-Out Burger ever offered a buy-one get-one free deal for a Double-Double? These businesses may offer a free menu item to support a cause, or they may give a percentage of total sales for a night to a school booster club or local charity, but I cannot remember a time that they ever played discount games with their regularly offered menu. They simply do not have to.

Sometimes these discount shenanigans can come across as "desperate for business." How many times have you placed an order for an item online and, as you checkout, they offer you an additional two items for a dollar? The flashing graphic says, "Add these two items to your cart within the next thirty seconds to save 99% off the price you just paid." It makes you question: how can they sell these items this deeply discounted and the original order at a much higher price? These strategies make the retailer look at least unscrupulous, and maybe even somewhat crooked, when you stop to think about the price differences offered.

We should always offer our services and products with honor. Never guilt anyone into patronizing a business. I try to avoid the appearance of desperation at all costs. It is just not a good look. I am sure everyone has seen the "Going Out of Business" banners. They look desperate for you to keep them afloat with your one purchase. It is just a bad business model to depend on. We have always priced our products fairly, treated people kindly, and consistently executed our service to our fullest ability. We have continued to stay busy offering those great products that people want. No games. No gimmicks. We are not selling a cheap product, and quality comes at a higher price. People who understand this are happy to pay a little more for a consistent quality product. I see no reason to diminish our product by offering it with questionable discounted pricing methods.

We recently celebrated our five-year anniversary, and I only had two people ask what we were doing for a special and if we had any discounts. I told them that we are already priced extremely fair for the ranch-to-table quality we offer. Neither seemed to have an issue with our prices. We had a solid day of sales without losing a dollar to a gimmick that could have hurt more than help. At Wells, there are no discount games needed.

Give them quality. That's the best kind of advertising.
~ Milton Hershey

The Rules of the Range

MANY BOOKS HAVE been written about business culture, and several specifically about restaurant culture. I am not going to rehash all their work, but I would like to say that culture may be one of the strongest factors we control within our restaurant.

The culture of a business has a few key points of traction when we look at it from a high level. I believe an effective restaurant culture must be centered around the team concept. On the ranch, we learn to depend on our fellow hands. We must trust other riders to be where we need them to be when herding cattle. There is no time to explain where another rider should be riding. It takes a team to move a group of cattle along to their destination, and everyone is responsible for riding in his spot and doing his job.

Waiters essentially work for themselves since their care for the customer generally determines their tip amount. However, if they consider themselves as part of a greater team, they could most likely make more in tips and contribute to the overall success of the entire restaurant. I really hate to see waiters in a busy restaurant with tunnel vision. They may not be your assigned waiter, yet they walk past your table carrying a full pitcher of tea and ignore that every tea glass on your table is empty. How great would it be for them to stop on their way and save their fellow waiter a trip back with the same pitcher? When everyone on staff works together for the restaurant, it makes a big difference; but when they are there only for themselves, it can be detrimental to the overall level of service the restaurant provides. While we are on the subject of tea glasses, why do some restaurants use such small glasses? Smaller glasses require more trips for the waiter to keep a customer happy, but I digress. The cowboy is always looking to help his compadres because he never knows when he will need that help himself.

Another great attribute of cowboy culture is the love of the land and appreciation for all things pertaining to life. The cowboy loves his horse and everything that is needed to take care of his steed. He has respect for his saddle and the leather he holds in his hands every day. He cares for the land and everything it produces in his life. A cowboy depends on these things and appreciates them down to the boots that protect him from snakebites and keep his feet dry in the mud. He understands it takes every element in his life to make his life beautiful.

Many business cultures seem to lack this basic appreciation of life. For that matter, it seems like many in our generation lack this appreciation in general. The more appreciation we have for life and its basic elements, the better we act and react in both life and business. It helps us become aware of those around us and appreciate them every day. It causes us to care about more than just ourselves. This culture of caring for others has been a cornerstone at our restaurant since day one. We appreciate every customer that comes through our doors. It is hard to genuinely care for people if you do not really care if they are there or not. When we truly appreciate life, it shows in the way we talk and in the way we act. It is easy to feel welcome when someone is appreciated.

Finally, a drive for excellence is crucial to the cowboy culture. Cowboys are driven to do things right simply because it is the right thing to do! When a horse is being trained, for instance, daily consistent dedication is required in order to see the results he is hoping to see. It takes a drive for excellence to wake up early and put the work in when nobody is looking.

In the restaurant business, there is more work behind the scenes than out front. The excellence from behind the kitchen doors will always be evident on the plate. Those hours spent in preparation before the doors are opened will be on display throughout the entire day of business.

The culture of the old Texas cowboy lives on in the way we treat others, work hard, and appreciate those who make our dreams come true every day. These fundamentals power our restaurant and empower our customers to speak well of us, continuing to support us year after year.

We're all in this together, Partner!
~ Woody, Toy Story

Ranch horse named Dunny.

Chapter Five
REIMAGINING RESTAURANTS

Overcoming the Negative

THERE ARE TELL-TALE signs within our society that give us insight into the way people think. We can watch social media and pick up on patterns and identify trends that can help us brace for changes and equip us to do our best. One of these trends that we have seen in recent years is the phrase, "Did not disappoint." We see this phrase when people are happy with their experience, but it is almost a double negative. I always think, when I read that phrase, "So you went into that business expecting to be disappointed?" How sad that our baseline emotion and standard expectation is disappointment! Because I see this all the time it seems that it is the collective expectation of many.

As a business owner, I need to know what to expect when new customers walk in. The only way to win them over is to work on changing this negative expectation from the moment they walk in. We do not want them disappointed with their service, their meal, or any other facet of their visit. At least we know the baseline and starting point, and we know we must prove them wrong by giving them the best experience they never saw coming.

It is a sad day to live in when this negativity rules our social media, review posts, and even our verbal conversations. Yet it is understandable when we experience the lack of care in many establishments today. In days gone by, people seemed to take pride in their work. They would work hard to keep their name and reputation good for all to see. However, these days so few seem to care. And here is the point of this seemingly negative discussion: in this environment, it is actually easier to be successful! You know the old cliche, "The darker the night, the brighter the light!" It has never been easier to stand out than right now. Simply be better than you are expected to be. When we strive to be the best we can be, the outcome is usually bright.

I hope there have been some ideas in this book that have encouraged you to make some small changes that might bring about some big results.

It really does not take that much effort to show people you care. A handshake or a "Thank you" goes so far these days. A simple heartfelt check-in at the table speaks volumes to the customer who is expecting to be disappointed yet again by another uncaring establishment. Prove them wrong! Try your best never to let them be disappointed.

We all lived through the crazy Covid shutdown, then the journey back, and finally the supply-chain issues that plagued us and still cause an occasional issue even today. It was a horrible time in our world, and restaurants had seemingly insurmountable odds to fight in order to stay open. It was an ongoing struggle to simply make a product and keep the doors open. I understand the struggle, and those who made the best of that bad deal were those who creatively solved those daily problems.

While we continued to serve our normal menu, we added family meals to our daily dinner menu. We turned our back dining room into an assembly kitchen and sold different meals each night of the week. Our tagline sounded like a TV dinner ad from the 1970s, "Just pop them in a hot oven and enjoy." We still get the occasional request for some of those dishes. We ran an advertising campaign that showed us throwing a roll of toilet paper into each bag. (Remember the great toilet paper shortage of 2020?)

The shutdown gave us an opportunity for creativity and innovation, and many thrived during this time of general hardship. But sadly, many used it as an excuse to do less. And here we are some three-plus years past the unfortunate time we faced with many still making excuses for why they do not have certain menu items. Some restaurants are still operating on scaled-back menus and abbreviated hours of operation because they got away with it during a hard time. They found it easier to stay the mediocre course rather than return to the establishment they once were. I will even say this: shame on those who have kept the bar low and worn out the same tired excuses when we have been given a new day to achieve so much more!

It seems that amidst adversity the passionate thrive, while the apathetic make excuses. We cannot ever afford to settle for an excuse-laden mindset. Our customer family deserves so much more. Let their love for us rekindle that passion that drove us to step out and begin this journey in the first place.

Keep your eyes and your mind open. Don't be blinded by filters like fear, uncertainty, pessimism, and negativity.
~ Carlos Wallace

Why Open at All?

HAVE YOU SEEN a business open and know from day one it will probably be a miracle if it stays open for a year? Statistically speaking, most small businesses do not remain open for ten years. Most fail within their first-to-fifth year of operation. The current national average of restaurant failure is 60% within their first year, and a whopping 80% never make it to year five! There are several reasons for this, many of which have already been discussed in this book, but let us consider the probable root of this failure in this section.

Recently I watched a grand opening video on social media from a local business. I was interested to see what they were doing because the building is very large and in an amazing location. It is a multi-million-dollar facility. They are set up to sell home medical supplies such as walkers, crutches, bandages, and specialty shoes. I am not an expert in this field; however, my analytical brain is wondering how much that lease runs a month, and how many crutches one must sell to make ends meet. I do not see how that business idea can be profitable. All these items can already be delivered directly or picked up from a local drug store. Many elderly people have them sent to their door via Medicare and Medicaid providers. Just because someone has an idea does not mean it will work, though I do wish these people the best!

I have watched candle shops open in our downtown area. The owners must pay massive rent for their space, and then they close in a matter of months. I understand that people like candles, but I would not want to be responsible for four thousand dollars a month in rent plus overhead costs when a fifteen-dollar candle is my method of profit. It is an idea, but not a solid business plan.

The same is true for restaurants. Many open but have no real means of making the business work. So many restaurants open without a real difference to offer their community. They are not offering a unique menu, better quality products, or a new approach of any kind. In my experience, a business needs to loudly trumpet its unique reason for existing. What specialty is being done better than other restaurants around the corner? What is the big idea that will propel you to the top of the water cooler conversations around town? What means of belonging do you offer to provide enough income to cover all costs and taxes and still make a profit?

I would never open a restaurant in an area without a specific purpose for being there. For us, there are several very important things that cause us to stand out: our ranch-raised whole-ground beef, house-made desserts and sauces, gluten-free and allergen-safe handling, and our down-home hospitality. These are things most chain restaurants cannot or do not offer. For that matter, most local establishments seem to take a generic approach to their menu, using staple items like dry gravy mixes, pre-formed patties, and generic frozen desserts. While this may work in a small town where there are no other choices, it does not seem to be a good business plan for a more populated area with plenty of restaurant options within driving distance. To add one more factor, an area must be able to handle the price point of your product offering. Not every city can sustain fine dining, for example. The customer base must be willing to spend the money for a concept to work long-term.

So why even open? What are you going to be able to offer your community that people cannot get down the street? What can you do better than anyone else? How are you going to make an ever-increasing payroll and other overhead expenses each month? You must be unique. You must stand out. You must serve with hospitality and love in order to prosper in this world. You must be the best you can be every day!

Sustainability is a word the restaurant world loves and rightfully so. However, the first element of sustainability does not pertain to tomato plants or lettuce suppliers. It is a business plan! As I mentioned earlier in this chapter, the failure statistics for the food and beverage industry are dismal. This was true even before the complications brought on by the pandemic and rising inflation. The simple reality is that restaurants are in an easy-fail position. Margins now are thinner as compared to most industries. Our supply prices vary with the weather and other availability factors. However, if our menu prices move up too much, our customers raise a commotion. Then the uproar on social media commences along with reviews that mention how "pricey" our menu has become.

Let me throw a shocker at you. Perhaps it is not the most quoted reason that small businesses fail. However, I submit to you that one of the biggest factors of failure in any business operation, even with a solid business plan, is an over/under estimation of your ability to earn money.

Let me explain it with a simple word problem. Everyone loved those in school. (Excuse the sarcasm.) Joe wants to open a tractor dealership. Right now, Joe works for someone else and lives on a $100,000 per year salary. Joe says to his wife, "I can make $100,000 a year selling tractors. It will be easy since I can make $10,000 per sale! Anyone can sell ten tractors in a year. Right?" That is less than one tractor per month.

However, when you work for yourself, you remove yourself from the umbrella of corporate employment and now find you are standing in the storm of self-employment penalties; or what politicians call *taxes*. This means you now keep much less of what you earn. What looks like on the surface to be ten tractors could very easily take selling fifteen to get back to the initial $100,000 goal, according to my sources. Also, this example uses Texas numbers. If you are in a state like California, you may need to sell twenty tractors to reach your net goal.

Why am I saying all of this? Because it takes so much more business to make a living than we ever account for in our startup plans. It jeopardizes many small businesses before they ever get off the ground, especially restaurants!

So how does a restaurant sell more than they expect to sell? How do you make your idea work? You need to be special. You need a specific reason for existing. You need to provide something that makes people excited to come see you.

We ate at home almost all the time when I was young. Actually, in the '80s, I think most people ate at home more than we do now. But when the rare occasion arose to go out to eat for dinner, it was a big deal. It was exciting. Where would we go? What kind of food? Could we maybe have a fountain drink or a shake? Boy, life was simpler back then. Nowadays we eat in restaurants many meals each week. Life has almost reversed roles from my childhood. Now I am excited to stay home and eat, rather than go out somewhere. And I believe that is at least partially because of the mediocre quality of most restaurants today.

However, there are a few places that still get me excited to visit where I can enjoy a delicious meal. I can still feel that twinge of excitement that we have reservations for a certain place for dinner, and I find myself looking forward to the occasion with anticipation of a favorite meal just waiting for me at seven o'clock this evening. It does not even have to be an expensive restaurant with a reservation to get me excited. There are a few restaurants right now that we frequent that I get excited about. There is a barbeque restaurant that has a special one day a week. When their special aligns with my schedule and I make plans to go there is that twinge of excitement and anticipation again! When we travel to certain places on vacation and we are close to a favorite restaurant that we have grown to love over the years, I get excited to go back! There are special entrees and even some side dishes that are exciting. One that comes to mind for me is the pass-around potatoes at Lambert's. Everyone else is excited about "throwed rolls," but stop by my table every time you have that pot of soft-fried potatoes!

We should all strive to have items on our menu so fantastic and consistent that we create excitement within people when they come to enjoy them with us. Just a few weeks ago I was working on Saturday, which is my custom. As we were opening, I reached into the window to turn on the open sign and saw a man stand up from the driver's side of a van. I recognized that stretch, and then I recognized the family. They had been driving for several hours that morning already.

They moved several states away for work a couple of years ago, and they said when they came in that Wells was their first stop in town. They timed their driving to get to us early to beat the line and get one of their favorite burgers! They had not found another burger to compare in the years they have been gone, and so before seeing family, before unpacking at the hotel, they had to get their exciting meal fix that they were looking forward to. What an amazing honor when we can affect a person's life and family in such a powerful way!

Once a business finds its reason for being, its greatness naturally flows from its passion and ongoing dedication to serving those who continue to return. It is then destined to make it!

The best way to find yourself is to lose
yourself in service of others.
~ Mahatma Gandhi

The Money-Centric Mindset

IN BUSINESS, WE must remain diligent to keep up with the financial shifts we encounter in our economy. We should never ignore the bottom line; however, it is possible to become hyper-focused on the margins and drive ourselves out of business. If you are scratching your head right now, good. We need to think about *money* and *service* differently. Countless books, podcasts, and lectures have been published over the years about protecting profit margins and managing the hard costs associated with business. My fear is that in small businesses some owners may take it too far, even to a place of zero profit or bankruptcy. Yes, margins can be thin in small businesses. However, if managing margins becomes the primary focus of your business, something is already wrong. At this point, there is another problem somewhere that must be found and addressed.

The old saying is true, "It takes money to make money." Most times, it takes an outlay of money before a profit is ever made. However, being cheap is counterproductive to the establishment of a loyal customer base. My philosophy has been: I would rather spend money to provide superior quality, than pinch every penny to the place of being left with an inferior product. I have seen more than one restaurant cheapen their ingredients to the point where their food was not worth serving. Now I am not suggesting that every ingredient must be flown in fresh from its country of origin. However, underspending seems to be a more prevalent practice than overspending. So, within reason, I try to buy the best ingredients possible wherever I can, thus creating the best products served, even if it costs more than many others might pay. When companies "go cheap" on everything due to the profit margins, it becomes impossible to provide quality products at the price the customer is charged.

We could save multiple thousands of dollars each year if we ordered beef from a wholesaler like most everyone else does; but while it would help the bottom line, it would wreck our quality and rob us of our primary purpose for existing.

I was told by a friend and restaurant owner that we could save a great deal of money if we switched from #1 baker potatoes for our fries to the cheapest potatoes. His theory was since we are using them for fresh-cut fries, the shape does not matter. However, those potatoes also had other issues to reconcile. We found the lower quality potatoes also contain more starches and will not cook the same as the premium potatoes. So after one order of those cheaper potatoes, we decided our quality is more important than saving money.

Another trap restaurants fall prey to is the serving of smaller portions. There should be a standard value of food offered for the fair price you are selling it for. If the general public cannot get full with the portions that are served, then it should be called a "small plate," or it should be priced according to size with a reasonable upgrade option available.

There is a small diner in our area that has good-tasting food. We stopped in a couple of times while passing by during lunchtime, and neither time did we get full. The portion size was very small, while the price was higher than expected. If my memory serves me correctly, we spent close to $40 for two lunches and left hungry. It is hard to be a returning customer when this happens. I understand that food cost is high, but it does not matter how much profit you make once. If it cannot be repeated and spoken highly about, then it is a losing operation. I would venture to guess that overall, more money is made in the world through smaller margins and higher volumes than through larger profits with fewer sales.

It is much easier to build a customer base with quality products and fair portions. It is almost impossible to convince people to buy a cheap product. Unfortunately, higher prices are normal today due to inflation so we must give the customer everything we can to make their visit memorable and worthy of returning.

The concept of Wells is to give more than expected. We do this every day in several ways that may not be flashy or even noticed by everyone. I have noticed at other restaurants that when a cheeseburger is ordered as a double-meat burger, many times the cheese is left as a single slice. We decided from day one, that when someone doubles the meat, we double the cheese without even asking, and without charging any more for the extra slice of cheese. It is just a small thing we do to make our service that much better. To me, as the designer and chef, it seems that if a single meat cheeseburger gets one slice of cheese, then when the meat is doubled, the cheese must move up in ratio to match the same flavor and cheese quantity as the single. But as I just mentioned, most restaurants will charge for a second slice of cheese.

We also offer our five different house-made sauces. Many restaurants have started charging for such sauces. This trend started with the fast-food chains, but now it seems all types of restaurants are charging for the extra side of ranch or other sauce. We simply will not charge for our sauces. It is an extra value we want the customer to enjoy with us. If we were money-centric, sauces would be an easy upcharge item, but we would rather share our house-made goodness with our customers and enhance the value of their visit than make an extra fifty cents. It comes down to our desire to focus on quality and customer experience over making money.

Recently I read that back in the 1950s the automaker Volvo developed the three-point seatbelt technology that we have all grown so accustomed to in our vehicles. Volvo patented this technology first but decided to leave the patent open for all other vehicle manufacturers to use. While they could have made many millions on the patent, they felt that some things are better left free for all to benefit. While seatbelt safety, and the millions of lives saved, are not the same thing as a free menu item, I do agree that some things are better left free to enjoy. It just seems like the right thing to do.

Here in Texas when we go out for Tex-Mex food, we *expect* chips and salsa at the table when we sit down. It is part of the culture of Tex-Mex dining. It is fun, delicious, and a required part of the dining experience. I heard of a Mexican restaurant that decided to charge for their basket of chips and salsa. The owners said that their concept was more authentic than other Tex-Mex restaurants in town. You should have seen the uproar on social media! People's language was colorful as they vowed never to return until they offered complimentary chips and salsa. It was not long before the restaurant rectified their mistake and apologized for their folly. Some things should simply remain free for the benefit of the dining experience.

We have several free add-ons within our menu. Most places charge extra for grilled mushrooms, but now many are even charging for grilled onions! We will add either one of them to a burger without an additional charge. The same is true for green chilies, sauerkraut, and jalapeños. We simply want the customer to get everything they want on their burger for the price listed. It is our way of saying money is second and the customer is number one!

It has been my strong belief that when the focus is on the customer and the quality of their experience, money will take care of itself. If we make the best food possible as consistently as we can, and then treat everyone as if they are enjoying a burger at our home on the ranch, we will never have to pinch pennies and cut costs to the place where the customer and food quality suffer. We are determined never to become money-centric!

The best things in life aren't things.
~ Art Buchwald

What is Success?

THE TEXTBOOK DEFINITION of success is "the accomplishment of an aim or purpose." However, everyone knows true success is not just a single accomplishment, but a series of continual accomplishments achieved on a regular basis. It also seems that success should ultimately be determined by oneself, regardless of the opinions of others. But we should be able to agree on a few obvious successes for the purpose of our final discussion of this book.

To begin, we need sufficient sales to pay our overhead and have some left over for ourselves and our family. We must first achieve this level of success before we can move on to any others. We need to be successful enough to remain open for another week, another month, another year.

One of our first recognizable successes was the winning of several local community awards. The awards are great. However, as I have mentioned before, the beauty of these awards is their source. The community voted that we had the very best burger in the entire county! I will never forget our first Best Burger award. It was Christmastime of our first year. We had opened our doors on Labor Day, and our community hosted a "Best Of" poll on one of the large Facebook groups a week or two before Christmas of that first year. We had been open for about four months when we were nominated in the category for "Best Burger in Rockwall County." Our downtown area has several great burger restaurants. When I say that, I mean more than most communities our size. One local favorite has been a family serving burgers from their garage since 1967. One great burger comes from a restaurant owned by an internationally trained culinary chef who is very good at what he does. He owns a highly respected restaurant a couple of blocks from our location. Then there is another legitimate burger restaurant a couple of blocks in the other direction where the owner grinds his own brisket for burgers daily. Then there is a new large Dallas-Fort Worth burger chain that came to town boasting of some big-time burger awards.

The results of the public polls were to be announced at the local Christmas party. I really did not expect to win, but the competition came down to us and the famous local burger served from the garage. These guys are legends in our town. They were featured on several television shows and won more awards than they even remember since 1967. We had been open for four months. When they announced that the year's best burger in Rockwall County was Wells, I had to choke back a tear. There is a cell phone video of this announcement with me walking up to the stage wiping my eyes. I will never forget that night. That first accolade from our community said we served the number-one favorite burger in the county! Wow! I still get a little emotional thinking back on that special night.

The next year, groups within the community made extra efforts to ensure their favorite hamburger would win the top spot. But even with the extra awareness, Wells still brought home the trophy the second year from the Community Christmas party awards. The next year the Christmas Party was canceled due to Covid restrictions, and for some reason, the tradition was not carried into the third year. So, are we successful? Being recognized for our efforts is always a great feeling, but these are temporary wins and only as good as the day they are enjoyed. The following Monday we were right back in the kitchen working on consistency and quality as we always do.

We have gone on to win many awards since that first one, and have lost count of the number of polls, neighborhood favorites, and newspaper and magazine contests we have won. A popular Dallas magazine conducts an annual community survey and has named us Best Burger every year since opening. We are always just as honored as we were the first year! Then once again every Monday we are back at work trying to do better this week than we did last. I would say that community awards and accolades are a credible type of measurement of continued success, or at least a marker to be acknowledged along the way.

Another success marker that we consider is how well our "word of mouth" advertising is propagating organically. The best advertisement is the recommendation of a friend. We have heard some amazing stories of people being told to come eat at Wells. A man walked into the restaurant one day and said he was from South Carolina. He mentioned to someone prior to the business trip that he was flying to Dallas, and that person (in South Carolina) told him, "When you get there, you have to drive out to Rockwall and enjoy a Wells burger." He made the drive and loved his food. We had a great conversation. But can you imagine this local burger restaurant in a downtown suburb of Dallas being mentioned that many miles away? Such a cool happening!

We are greatly honored when customers bring their out-of-town family and guests to eat at our place. They say, "Wells is as Texan as it gets!" And that is a powerful message of success when our customers rave about our business and then bring their friends to visit.

Another measure of success is how many requests we receive to expand into other areas of the Metroplex and even other parts of Texas. I believe we have been officially invited to open a restaurant in every surrounding city. We have been asked to open locations in more cities than I can count. It is such a great honor to be asked, and it is some measure of success simply to be invited to join a new community.

One very important measure of success is community trust. When a business gains the trust of a community, it shows their belief in you. The importance you hold in their lives is put on display, and that may be one of the highest honors given to a business.

There are several ways a business can build trust in a community. One is to do what you say that you will do. Adhering to posted hours of operation is a simple way to build trust, and nothing breaks a business' trust like not being open when you said you would be open. Generous people may give you a second or third chance, but most may never give a business another chance when this happens. People understand legitimate reasons for business interruptions such as utility outages and weather closings, but simply not to be open when a business should be is an awful breach of trust.

Another way to build trust is to keep menu prices fair and consistent. Prices should not be constantly fluctuating. Price adjustments may be necessary every year or two, but not on a regular basis. Many families budget to go out to eat, and higher prices are not the kind of surprises people enjoy. The best way to convey trust is through simple consistency. Do the things that good businesses do every day and watch the level of trust build over time. It has been amazing to watch our customers come to our defense over the years. We work hard to be trustworthy in the sight of each customer.

When my older daughter was a sophomore in high school, she took piano as one of her electives. As she was preparing for her end-of-year recital, I shared a little Dad wisdom. As a bass player for many years, I had been used to holding down the beat with the band drummer. I explained to her that everyone misses notes sometimes, but you can never stop playing simply because you make a mistake. That evening she missed a big note during her performance, but she kept her timing and floated right over the mistake. It was noticeable but not memorable to those listening. When she had struck the final note, she received one of the longest and loudest applauses of the evening.

Her performance was spectacular, especially for a tenth-grade student. For those who may be curious, she performed an amazing rendition of *Skyfall* by Adele. I still have that performance on my phone some five years later. It was the consistency of the rhythm that kept the audience's trust throughout the performance even though a mistake was made. In business, mistakes are made, but we cannot afford to allow them to stop our progress. We must strive for consistency to continue to build the trust of our customers.

The marker of success that I never anticipated is the realization that we are redefining what a great burger really is. When we opened our doors, we had a couple of simple hopes. First, we wanted people to like our food, and second, we wanted people to come back again and help keep us open another week. We never imagined that we would hear people say, "It is different now when we eat burgers anywhere else since we have had your burgers here." Wow! I will always remember the first time a customer said this to me. He had been to another large city and had a burger at a big-name celebrity chef's burger restaurant. When I asked him how he liked it, he told me that it was all right, but it was nothing compared to the one in his hand as he was eating one of our burgers. That blows my mind, but I have heard it hundreds and maybe thousands of times since then. We could have never anticipated causing a seismic shift in the culinary world of burgers.

As I am thinking of this right now, I am slightly embarrassed saying it. But it is true. It is a real thing that we have witnessed happening. As I have mentioned before about my recent trip to Las Vegas, we too tried burgers from a celebrity burger restaurant. The fries were perfect; the service was great; the restaurant was immaculate; and everything was exactly as it should be. However, as perfect as everything was, the beef in the burgers paled in comparison to Wells' whole-ground beef. The flavor of the beef just did not compare. I would never insult this chef by mentioning his name. I have the highest level of respect for him and his culinary ability, along with his other successes in life; but our beef is simply better. I would humbly prepare him a burger to show him the difference in our beef. And here is how much confidence I have in his palette: he would most likely agree.

So, what is success? I have mentioned a few markers of successful days or seasons. However, regardless of what success we have seen to this point, none of that is promised to us tomorrow. We must wake up every day and press for another great day. We need another winning week and another successful month. When we get to the end of our journey, we will be able to look back and see that with all the successes we have enjoyed, it really did take making food that people liked. And we needed them to come back again and again to continue to keep us open for another week.

There is always a yearning to achieve more.
I'll continue to climb, trying to reach the top,
but no one knows where the top is.
~ Chef Jiro Ono

Lee Wells on his horse, One Eye

CHAPTER SIX
CLOSING TIME

The Semblance of Ease

MANY TIMES, WHEN we watch others from the outside, success can appear easily obtained. That mindset is always a trap. Social media can trap us in a world where everyone's life looks great until we realize they are only showing us the good days, the best angle of their face, and the happiest events of their life. There is a great deal of *real life* we never are allowed to see on a social media account.

As I was completing this manuscript, I asked a handful of close friends and family to pre-read the book and give me honest feedback. One of the first comments was that I may have made the journey sound too easy. I did not write about the details of every hard night and every bad day we struggled through. So, I felt the need to close the book with this chapter which I could have called, "A Small Dose of Reality."

If you have ever watched a pro football game from the safety of your living room couch, those trained athletes really do make their job look easy. But the more you understand their physical conditioning, years of extensive training and grueling hard work, everything falls into perspective. With their size and their speed, they can make normal people's heads spin in real life. If you are ever on the field to see how talented a quarterback must be to send the football past five or six men trying to knock it down or intercept it, you will understand the skill required to make it happen. It may look easy on the big screen, but it is extremely difficult at the speed of real life.

While I would never compare our restaurant to a professional sports team, nor would I equate myself or our staff with the likes of professional athletes, I do know the work that goes into each day of our business to make it the establishment I am writing about. I am well aware of the long hours it takes to make this business work, the struggles in the kitchen, and the delicate balance of customer service when the customer is upset. I know the constant mental awareness that I carry every waking moment of my life. The weight is simply always there without escape.

I apologize if somehow this book seems to minimize the struggle of operating a small business. If I did that somehow, it was unintentional. Nothing in this life is easy! If we succeed at all, it is in spite of all of the rules and regulations that seem to be designed to make business harder. Our country has grown so dependent upon the taxes of small businesses that the government seems okay with choking every inch of growth we seem to gain. I could go on about the current inflation and supply issues that may remain for years to come. In no way would I try to minimize the struggle of operating a small business in our generation.

Nothing worth obtaining is going to come about easily. Success comes through a determined, consistent effort that recognizes that failure is not an option.

I mentioned the Covid shutdown in a couple of places within the book. The shutdown was a challenging time. Our limits were tested, but we fought back with such tenacious determination that we grew through the process. We remodeled our entire restaurant! Was it easy? No way! But we found a way not only to survive but also to grow and improve. At one point, I was receiving several emails a week concerning the second round of government assistance, so I contacted my certified public accountant and asked him if we somehow qualified. After researching my question for a couple of days, he called me to explain that we had to have a loss over a certain time during the shutdown. When I asked him what our numbers were, he said that we had actually gained momentum during that time and did not qualify for the assistance. He said we had increased our profits every month of the time in question! That is not easy! I am not sure we had ever worked so hard. But we were determined to succeed.

Most small business owners have had people walk out on them mid-shift. We have had supplies back ordered or repair companies that could not get to us until next week. We have had that negative customer who would not be consoled. We may have experienced scathing reviews from phone notifications during a date with our spouse. The list could go on and on.

Hardship usually accompanies success. It is to be expected. It is impossible to do anything in physics without friction. Friction is a constant, just as negativity is in business. But I choose not to focus my time and energy on the bad when so much greatness surrounds me.

I hope you have enjoyed the variety of quotes throughout the book. I will leave you with one final quote to ponder. I have searched for years to find the original author. I do not believe it is original with me, but I guess that is possible. The quote is, "Shakespeare worked without knowing he would become Shakespeare." I believe ol' Bill might be a little taken aback to see every high school and university still studying his works after several centuries. We all live our lives and work at what we feel is important, but we cannot ever fully understand the impact we have on others.

We work hard to create great food, but we also desire to impact people in a deeper way than just providing another meal. For example, acts of kindness and an attitude of gratefulness influence others long after the meal is over. We opened a burger business without knowing what it would ultimately become. We had no idea that our customers would say that we have shifted what a good burger is to them. We never expected to win numerous awards, and we never realized we would hear people say, "This is the best burger we have ever had!" Yet we continue to hear it every day. As we press forward with the Wells culture of excellence, we know that our history is still being written.

Thank you for picking up this book. Thank you for reading these pages. I sincerely hope something I said encourages you to reach higher and see greater days. Feel free to reach out to me on social media and send your thoughts about the book. I would love to hear from you!

Lee E. Wells

The End. (for now)

Lee Wells, Owner & Author

Next Steps

Request a Meeting or Speaking Engagement:

As a keynote speaker and an entrepreneur for twenty-plus years, Lee enjoys speaking to groups of all sizes about business culture, and he also allows some time for business consulting. Please send questions, feedback, or requests directly to: author@wellscattleco.com.

Continue the Conversation:

Lee hosts a weekly business podcast called: The Ranch & Table. You can find it anywhere you watch or listen to your favorite podcasts. Stay tuned for Lee's upcoming book!

Milton Keynes UK
Ingram Content Group UK Ltd.
UKHW041217281123
433415UK00003B/14/J